REELING IN THE PRAISE

"In Kevin Walsh's book, a simple weekend fishing trip becomes an occasion for an aging father and his three sons to rediscover how much they love each other."

—Rabbi Harold Kushner
author of *When Bad Things Happen to Good People*

"Kevin has done it again. He always finds a way to use sports as a backdrop to bring people together. *The Perfect Catch* is a warm story that will touch you."

—Jim Nantz

"For any man who has ever wanted to make his father proud and bond with his brothers, you must read *The Perfect Catch*. It's perfect for anyone who loves the outdoors, loves to fish and is not afraid to put love back into the tricky dynamic of male relationships in the family and among friends."

—Dr. Marty Becker
"America's Veterinarian"

"Fathers and sons and rods and reels and heartbeats in rhythm. Read *The Perfect Catch.*"

—Dan Shaughnessy
author, *Francona, the Red Sox Years*

"Any woman who has ever doubted that women create relationships while men solve problems will have some aha moments with this book! Great fun, and good info. I'm hooked. You will be, too."

—Mary M. Mitchell
bestselling etiquette author of *Complete Idiot's Guide to Etiquette, Fast Track*, and 7 other books including *Woofs to the Wise: Learning to Lick at Life and Chew on Civility*

"Just so you know, the Kevin Walsh I once knew melted crayons in my sink and was totally fascinated with creating a mohawk hair tall tale doll with the classroom sewing machine. How he became a TV guy and author I'll never know, but I'm sure proud of him."

—Lorraine Hirsh
Kevin's Fifth Grader Teacher, Rydal Elementary

"A man's book written by a boy whom I taught along with his brothers many years past. 'Who'd a thunk it?' Nice going, Kevin."

—Robert Hunter
Kevin's Sixth Grader Teacher, Rydal Elementary

"This book has soul."

—Gary Tanguay
Screenwriter and Sports Tonight TV Host, Boston

the PERFECT CATCH

Stephanie,

Enjoy the book and lead Rydal well.

Kevin Walsh

the PERFECT CATCH

Fishing, Family and Friendship

KEVIN WALSH

Boston, Massachusetts

Paperback ISBN13: 978-0-9839012-5-9
Hardcover ISBN13: 978-0-9839012-6-6
Kindle ISBN13: 978-0-9839012-0-4
Library of Congress Control Number: 2013940184
Library of Congress Cataloging information on file with publisher.

Sweet Tea Books
PO Box 812748
Wellesley, MA 02482
www.SweetTeaBooks.com
www.Facebook.com/ThePerfectCatchBook

Design and production: Concierge Marketing, Inc.
Printed in the United States
10 9 8 7 6 5 4 3 2 1

For my father, brothers, wife,
and children and all those who fish.

Contents

Introduction: The Rabbi and the Catholic 1

1 Wetting the Fly, Whetting the Appetite 7

2 Meet My Dad, Bob 19

3 Coming Home 23

4 Meet My Older Brother, Chris 33

5 Four Guys Four Wheelin' 37

6 Meet My Younger Brother, Michael 45

7 It'll Be Better Fishing Where We're Going 49

8 Brothers Fight Over Beer—in Walmart 55

9 On Fish, Fish On! 59

10 Before Fly Fishing, Bats and Bricks to the Head 75

11 Good Guys, Great Fly Fishing Guides 89

12 Cell Phones Swim with the Fishes 97

13 90 Percent of Fish Are Caught by 10 Percent of Fishermen 101

14 Brothers Inside and Outside the River 115

15 Fish Out of Water, My Dad at a Bar 125

16 Meet My Mom, Carole 131

17 My New Mom and the Greatest Love Story Ever 147

18 The Perfect Catch 155

19 Tell Your Sons to Go Fishing 169

20 We're Screwed 175

21 The Healing Ride Home 187

22 Thanksgiving 201

23 Return to the Trout Pond and Promises of a Better Brotherhood 207

Thank You Note to Dad 219

Acknowledgments 221

About the Author 225

INTRODUCTION: THE RABBI AND THE CATHOLIC

It was early May 2012. Sitting across from me at a Panera Bread in suburban Boston with a cup of coffee between his hands was my friend and best-selling author Rabbi Harold Kushner. We get together every couple of months to talk about sports, life, and writing. On this day I wanted to tell him about my upcoming fly fishing trip with my dad and brothers and how special it was to us as men.

The rabbi wanted to know more about the fishing and my relationship with my family. I kind of expected he might ask, and I was more than willing to share.

I told Rabbi Kushner that my dad didn't give us much choice about whether we could make it. Dad more or less told my brothers and me that we would be joining him in six months and at his expense. It was a summons with plenty of advance notice, a call to action; and we obeyed. He's still our father after all. It turned out to be a perfect call.

Even though Dad lives in a different state, I see him about every other month. I can't say the same for my brothers. They live in two different states much farther away. There are stretches when I won't see my brothers for a couple of years. With four men living in four different states it isn't easy to get together. In fact, it had been five years since we last did, and more than *thirty* years since we piled into a car for an appreciable drive to a vacation destination.

In recent years we had discovered that fishing was something we could count on. It was an event. Let's face it, men need an event to get together. All the men in my family fish. Some do it more and better than others. The point is we enjoy it, and we enjoy doing it together. We needed this vacation. We needed to resolve some lingering issues—or at least I did. I was not as good of a brother as I should have been, and I wanted to fix that. But whether it was my intention, or someone else's, it was perfectly clear to everyone that we needed to be more involved in each other's lives, despite the great distance separating us.

This would be a first. We had never taken a guys-only family vacation. It felt wonderfully weird. The rabbi took it all in with a warm look on his face that matched the coffee in his hands. He's a good man and a great listener.

Rabbi Kushner wanted to talk about something else too. He was worried about his Boston Red Sox. He's a season ticket holder so he's invested. He watches me on TV talking about the state of Red Sox Nation, and he wanted to know more. It was only a month into the season, but already new manager Bobby Valentine was being crushed by fans and talk radio for his weird personality and questionable baseball decisions. The rabbi was wondering if the season was a lost cause. I hated to tell him, but it sure looked lost to me.

So how exactly do a rabbi and a good Catholic boy hook up? About ten years ago, while my wife, Jean, and I were living in Central California, she suffered a miscarriage. We were hurting.

A priest recommended reading *When Bad Things Happen to Good People* by Harold Kushner. If anyone could relate to a bad thing happening to a good person, it was Rabbi Kushner. He lost his twelve-year-old son Aaron to progeria, old man's disease. Rabbi Kushner's book gave me and, ultimately, Jean peace when we needed it most.

When I moved to Boston in the summer of 2009, I had remembered that Harold Kushner was from the greater Boston area. With the help of another rabbi whom I'd met at a book signing for my first book, *The Marrow in Me*, I tracked Harold Kushner down. I sent him one of my personal copies of *The Marrow in Me*. He read it, enjoyed it, and later reached out by email. We've been friends and coffee conversationalists ever since.

"You know, Kevin, it's very unusual for men to get together like we're doing," Rabbi Kushner said, mug in hand. "Men don't often get together as friends just for conversation. The women do, but if you ever see two men in a restaurant together, they're almost always talking about business. Look around," he suggested.

I observed two men sitting by the front door with a legal pad between them. Off to the side another man sat solo, fiddling with his pencil and looking out the window. No doubt he was awaiting the arrival of an associate.

Around the shop I noted small groups of women engaged in conversation leaning toward one another for closer connection and privacy—no barrier between them. Next to us a large group of women, members of a book club, had gathered at a table to discuss last month's novel and what to read next.

Rabbi Kushner's comment about the dearth of male bonding pointed out what should be obvious to all, but what so many men are oblivious to—we often ignore our fellow man, including those in our families. I was as sure of this as the rabbi was. But what you feel in your heart, gut, and soul sometimes needs academic muscle to do the flexing. So I picked up the phone and called two manly men who could do that kind of heavy lifting with appropriate credibility.

"It's true and a very significant phenomenon that runs very deep in our society with strong implications," says Boston College Professor and Neuropsychologist Joe Tecce. "Men rarely show compassion and bonding with each other unless it's behind the scenes, one-on-one. Showing concern for a fellow man is perceived as a weakness, and most men won't risk that."

"It wasn't always this way," says Dr. Anthony Rotundo, historian and author of *American Manhood*. "In the late 1800s you often saw boys and men on sports teams posing for pictures with their arms draped around each other's shoulders and leaning into each other.

"But around 1910 things started to change. Those same pictures became the ice cube tray model, a coolness toward whoever was next to you, and each in his own compartment. Connecting and bonding were discouraged. It starts early and accumulates over a lifetime in a toxic way. In the end men don't know how to nurture each other and take care of each other. They don't know how to listen to what a guy is saying and how to understand what he's *really* saying. There's a cost for that," according to Dr. Rotundo.

The cost is an emotional toll that taxes our health, our spirit, and our relationships. The short shrift isn't just limited to our male friends. We guys often do it to the men in our families too. And you know what? It's just so darn unnecessary. That's when I knew I had another book to write: a book for men about men, and one that the women seated next to Rabbi Kushner and me would want their husbands to read.

I hoped to accomplish a lot of things with the fishing trip and ultimately the writing, but for simplicity sake let me see if I can boil it down to about five. That's enough. More than anything, I'll admit very selfishly, I wanted to build a better relationship with my brothers. I hungered for what all sons crave—a father's approval. I wished for Dad to see how proud his sons are of *him* and how thankful we are for the lives and opportunities he's given us as we strive to become the good men, fathers, and friends we long to be. I hoped that readers would vicariously see a part of themselves in our family's stories so they too could reflect on building more caring relationships with the men in their lives. And lastly, I just wanted to have some reasonably clean good fun while being a man's man. That's good living.

Fishing would be the framework for my personal and family journey. But the male bonding and friendship beyond the bonds of blood would hopefully be the greater takeaway. That would only come with difficult self-introspection and letting go of self-absorption. The question was, would this trip give me the chance to make it right?

As far as the Red Sox go, there was no question about how bad they were in 2012. The not-so-loveable losers lost ninety-three games. It was their worst season in forty-seven years. They missed the playoffs for the third straight season. Manager Bobby Valentine was fired a day after the season ended.

Still, Rabbi Kushner believes. He thinks the team that so many people around Boston have given up on is worth fighting for. That's why he spends so much time going to games, watching them on TV, scouring the box score, and talking about it with guys like me. I believe that's called faith. And if the good rabbi can have it in the Red Sox, I can certainly have faith in my family.

ONE

Wetting the Fly, Whetting the Appetite

Author Kevin Walsh, Needham, Mass., 2012

It was just before sunset on a spectacular late October day in 2012 in Needham, Massachusetts. The daytime high hit 63 degrees, about 10 degrees above normal. As the sun fell, its low angle made the colors of the trees around the trout pond of the Needham Sportsman's Club pop. The water was as smooth as glass, capturing a perfect reflection of the orange, red, purple, and yellow leaves that would soon fall into the water and sink to the bottom.

As I sat on the tailgate of my white Toyota Tacoma pickup, I was thankful for many things in my life—my health and family in particular. I have a beautiful wife, Jean, who has blessed me with two darling, young daughters: eleven-year-old Samantha and nine-year-old Amanda. I was also thankful that I had a place like this to come to and thankful for the role that fishing plays in my life and the lives of my family members.

Thanksgiving was a month away, and I would join my elderly father and two adult brothers on a fishing trip of a lifetime in the tributaries of the Great Lakes in Western New York. Four men, living in four different states, gathering together for the first time in a long time, and what might be the last time. Much like the fish that we were going after, we too were going back to our roots.

Late fall is the time when steelhead trout swim out of the Great Lakes and up the rivers to lay their eggs in the same place where they were born. Side by side they swim, and side by side they spawn, spawning an opportunity to bond in an experience as profound for us as it is for them. As the fish hunker down in pairs in the channels of the river, we would pair up as partners trying to catch them. But this trip was not really about fishing. It was about us connecting as men, with fishing providing the vehicle.

Before we got to that stage, I still had a little fishing business to take care of at the Sportsman's Club in Needham. I slipped on my Orvis vest and carefully slid off the back of my truck. If there were fish in the front left corner of the pond, I don't want to let them know I was coming.

I stepped slowly and gently along the gravel that led up to the grassy bank lining the pond's edge. I saw a few risers, so I knew where to cast. I released the wooly bugger from where it was latched in a holding hoop near the bottom of the rod. The fly was olive green with red thread wrapped around its neck below a white head. If I were a fish, I think I'd take a bite.

I pulled some slack out of the reel to add line and weight. I lifted the rod tip to two o'clock and flicked my right wrist in the direction of eleven o'clock, letting the excess line slide through the fingers of my left hand. After a couple of back and forths, with the backcast nearly touching the clubhouse porch, I let the line go. The fly landed about twenty-five feet away and slowly sank into the dark water. I started a slow strip, inching the fly through the water toward me. No luck.

I lifted the fly out of the water and cast again, this time landing the wooly bugger about two feet to the right. On the second strip the lime green fly line and the foam strike indicator darted down and to the left. I lifted the rod tip up to the right and felt resistance. The unmistakable bounce in the line and the rod tip said "fish on."

Not wanting to give the fish any opportunity to slip off the hook, I lifted the rod straight up to set the hook deeper into the fish's lip. I took a deep breath and tried to calm my racing heart. I love the adrenaline rush of the strike and fight, but also the balance it takes to not "horse the fish." More than anything, I try to do less. I've lost more fish trying hard instead of trying easy. I held the rod tip up, knowing that doing so kept tension on the line and made the fish swim "uphill."

After a couple of jumps, zigs, and zags, the trout was tuckered out and ready to be reeled in. I switched the heavier fly line from my left hand to my right, pinching it up against the rod with my top two fingers while the bottom fingers squeezed the rod handle into the heel of my hand. After a couple of cranks with my left hand, the twelve-inch rainbow trout had surrendered. I reached down and plucked it out of the water. The fly was embedded in the corner of its mouth. It took a few wiggles to get it out. Once the hook was free, I set the fish free back in the water. I don't fish for food, fishing feeds my soul.

Thrilled by the catch, I couldn't wait to catch up with my dad and brothers on the phone, and I was hopeful we'd land a bunch more fish together Thanksgiving week. With that goal in mind I put my rod back inside the truck and went into the clubhouse to make a few calls. I also wanted a beer.

The clubhouse resembles a log cabin. It's just one room, about 600 square feet in size. There's a small kitchen with a refrigerator, sink, and gas stove for cooking. There's a wood-burning stove for heat, a few tables and chairs, and lots of pictures on the walls of fish caught by club members. Nothing fancy. It's just right. Nothing more, nothing less. Anyone could be comfortable here. I put two dollars in the honor system till, took a can of Heineken out of the fridge, and cracked it open.

I took a swig of beer while sliding my finger across my iPhone to unlock the screen. I hit the favorites star to bring up the list of names on speed dial. Bob Walsh is at the top. I touched his name to start the automatic dialing.

"Hello, Kevin," he answered with cheer in his heart, a cordless phone in one hand and raw materials for building a bamboo fly rod in the other.

"What are you doing Dad?" I asked.

"I'm building my bamboo fly rod for the trip. I've already built you boys your own rods with your names etched on the sides."

I don't know that I'd ever seen or heard my dad more geeked up about anything. He was so pumped for the trip. He is a fisherman's fisherman, but first and foremost a father. And he hadn't had his three adult sons together in five years. At seventy-three years of age, he knew he probably didn't have another five years of good enough health and stamina to plan another fishing trip.

So he took the liberty that comes with age and money. He booked and paid for the trip before even asking if his sons could make it. It was just the kind of positive pressure that made it happen. If he had said something back in the spring such as, "Check your availability for Thanksgiving week," someone would have wriggled out. No one did. We all understood that this might be it

"Dad, I caught a fish at the pond," I told him as I cradled the beer can in my hand.

"Really? How big?" he wanted to know.

"About a twelve-inch rainbow."

"Oh, that's great. But you'll catch much bigger ones where we're going. They can get up to thirty inches."

"Nice! Okay, Dad, gotta go. Love you. I'll see you in a couple of weeks. I'm gonna call Chris."

After I hung up, Dad went back to work on his fly rod in his Ledyard, Connecticut, basement workshop. He still had to plane the individual bamboo strips, glue them together, bake them inside a special oven, dip the rod in a tube of varnish, wrap the snake guides onto the bottom side, attach the reel seat, and glue on a cork handle. Got all of that? What you just read in fifteen seconds took about *sixty hours* in real time. This is the kind of work Bob Walsh lives to do, now that he's done with working for a living.

Dad is living the good life after forty years in the pharmaceutical industry. He's a fat cat, but prefers dogs. His nine-year-old Corgi, Annie, follows him around like he's the Pope. If you put a miter on Dad's head, he sort of resembles Pope John Paul II in his younger days, although his closest celebrity doppelganger is U.S. Senator and Astronaut John Glenn.

Dad worked his tail off and got it while the getting was good. But he worries about the corporate world his sons are working in. He's seen us all be laid off at one time or another and having to relocate our families. He hears us talk about trying to protect our jobs in a difficult economy. It's not that he didn't have struggles at different points in his career; he had to relocate once too. Now he readily admits, "I got out just in time."

As I finished off that first beer, I thought about the good place where Dad is at this stage of his life and whether I might be there someday too. He's seventy-three, happy and financially comfortable. It was a sobering thought, but the reality is, if I live as long as he has and have half the income then that he does now, I'll be damn lucky.

But at forty-two, I realize that I am lucky to have the life that I do already. I go to hundreds of professional sporting events including Super Bowls and Stanley Cup Finals, interview world-class players and coaches in the locker room afterward, and I talk about it on TV in the best sports town in the world. Most people I know can't believe I get paid to do this. Neither can I, but I'm glad I do.

I grabbed another beer and called my forty-four-year-old brother, Chris, in San Antonio, Texas. I caught him as he was leaving the office after a twelve-hour work day. That's actually a short day for him. The day before he had stayed until almost midnight.

"Yo, what's up?" Chris answered the phone in a Philly accent that doesn't quite fit in this land of Southern drawls.

He was walking out the back door of the wealth management division of a major bank, and he sputtered into the phone as he suffered the indignity of being attacked by a swarm of snub-nosed moths. It was as if someone on the roof had dumped a load of leaves on his head. It scared the crap out of him, but he knew it was funny. He chuckled as the swarm headed off to the south, on its way to Mexico for the winter migration.

As he balanced the phone on his ear, he climbed into his aircraft-carrier-sized Chevy Suburban. It's Texas; of course his car is big.

"I just caught a nice rainbow trout and I'm on my second beer," I told him.

"*You suck*," he said, saying each word slowly to intensify the insult and to reveal his envy. "How is it that you're fishing on a Tuesday and having a beer while the rest of the world is working?"

"Did you forget that I work on the weekends? While you and the rest of the world are relaxing and watching sports, people like me are covering it for people like you. Most people's work slows down, or stops on the weekend. Ours picks up. My Tuesday and Wednesday are your Saturday and Sunday."

"Fair enough," he conceded. "What else is going on?"

"Just enjoying the fishing here and looking forward to fishing with you guys next month."

"Yeah, me too. I need it," Chris said before saying goodbye.

It was an hour earlier in the central time zone and there was still a stitch of light outside. The light that was left illuminated the South Texas sky with a collage of red, orange, and purple colors. Chris's view outside his workplace was probably as stunning as the one I had at the trout pond in New England.

On his way home, Chris would pass the Steel Eel rollercoaster at SeaWorld rising and twisting in the colorful sky. It made him think of his three children, all of whom have been on the Eel and to SeaWorld for water shows many times. As kids, we three brothers would daringly go on roller coasters at Six Flags Great Adventure in Jackson, New Jersey.

Chris had a thirty-mile drive to Fair Oaks Ranch where his high-powered days started at 5:30 every morning. I'm sure as he settled in for the ride, thoughts of jumping steelhead and fighting brown trout filled his head and made the time fly. He would imagine himself catching trout in bunches and tilting beers with his brothers to celebrate. But reality might interrupt his fantasy as he would check in at home during his long drive.

He would call up his wife, Suzanne, this time on the Bluetooth technology planted in his ear. Chris loves the Bluetooth even though we brothers tell him he looks like a tool for wearing it.

"I don't care. It's easier to drive," he would tell us as if there's no other reasonable answer, and because it annoys us that he's not annoyed by our insult.

Chris's busy life rarely slows down, not with three active children and two dogs. He doesn't like surprises. That's a big reason why he always calls ahead. He wants to know what he's getting into once he gets home.

On this call, he told me later, he learned Suzanne and his fourteen-year-old daughter Caitlyn went to watch eight-year-old son Christopher's baseball practice. On the way home they picked up Little Caesar's pizzas. Coming home to pizza is always a party for Chris—even though his late work day and long drive would put him there after everybody else was done with dinner and getting started on their schoolwork. Everybody except for oldest son, Tyler. Chris would have to track him down.

Sixteen-year-old Tyler Walsh was at the golf course pounding balls on the driving range. He's a single-digit handicapper who plays for his high school team and on the American Junior Golf Association Tour. He hopes to play the PGA Tour someday. It's great to have high aspirations, but it's important to take care of high school just the same.

"Tyler, it's Dad. Stop hitting balls and go home and do your homework," Chris would command into his Bluetooth and through the cell phone that Tyler had pressed against his ear.

With Tyler successfully wrangled, Chris could put his focus back on I-10. About ten miles away from his Fair Oaks Ranch home, he would pass a road sign that read 530 miles to El Paso. He might think, *God that's far.* It sure is, but it's not as far away as Western New York where he would be in a month, counting his blessings, enjoying the bonds of brotherhood, and hopefully catching a lot of fish with his dad and brothers.

By the time Chris had probably pulled into his ranch home, I had just finished my second beer. I had one more call to make.

"Kev, I just got off a plane. What can I do for you?" thirty-five-year-old Michael Walsh asked while answering his cell phone as he walked off a flight at Hartsfield-Jackson Atlanta International Airport.

"Just checking in," I said. "How's it going? You excited about the trip?"

"Yeah," he sighed. "I could really use a break."

Mike is a research consultant. It's a good living, but a tough way to make one—a lot of time on the road and often on call. This fishing trip, in theory, should be the perfect way to get away.

We talked while he walked. Mike likes the long walk from the airport terminal to the parking lot. He's done it many times before. "It gives me time to think," he always says.

Mike was coming home from the New York metropolitan area where he made a presentation for a client in Teaneck, New Jersey. There was a lot of pressure on him, he confided in me. He was at the end of a ninety-day contract, having left his full-time job in July. If he did well, he might get a job offer out of it. The audience challenged him, but that was to be expected. There were parts about the presentation and Q and A that he felt really good about, and others that he wished he could have done better, he told me. This is the give and take of a demanding job. He was glad to be on his way home to Sandy Springs, Georgia.

After a ten-minute walk, he stuck his key into the driver's side door of his very feminine 2009 white Mini Cooper, which previously belonged to his wife, Rachel. After paying $18 for parking he would opt to take I-85 north, which took him up the gut of downtown Atlanta. It's not a straight shot. There are plenty of twists and turns with exciting views and temptations. He would pass Turner Field, the Georgia Statehouse, the campus of Georgia Tech, and the dormitories that housed Olympians in the 1996 Summer Games.

Each time he drives through the city he wrestles with himself about stopping for a chili dog at the famous food joint, The Varsity.

"I almost caved in. I really wanted one. Then I thought better of it and kept on driving," he admitted as we continued our phone conversation.

After he passed the world headquarters of Coca-Cola, the highway splits. Mike would stay left at the fork and merge onto Georgia 400. With the wider road and less traffic, he'd accelerate. When he would reach 75 miles per hour, he would click the cruise control button on the side of the wheel.

I heard a click on the phone line. "Kev, I gotta go. Rachel is clicking through on call waiting. I'll see you in a couple of weeks."

Rachel is Mike's wife of seven years and the mother of their two children, four-year-old Anne and Peter, age one.

I knew Mike's drive on 400 is a relatively straight one. It would give him time to reflect on what was a long day, and a possible new adventure in his professional life. Michael had been flying back and forth from Atlanta to New York regularly. The commute is rough and the contract work is very detailed and exceptionally challenging. Most couldn't do it. Mike can and does. It's his living. He has a young family that's counting on him.

The fishing trip with his brothers and dad couldn't come soon enough. On this day, he caught a podcast of *This American Life* on NPR. He was listening to Ira Glass narrating the story of Penn State being named the number one party school in America by the *Princeton Review*. He would later replay this for us on the long drive to the fishing grounds. It would remind us all of when we were younger.

I could picture Mike stopping to pick up the mail and with mail in hand and bag in tow, Mike would walk into his home. Georgia, a Doberman Pinscher mix would bark her greeting, his children would scream with joy, and Rachel would reach to relieve him of what he held in his hands. We should all be so lucky to have such a reception.

After dinner, Mike might relax after his raucous homecoming and think about how much of a break the upcoming fishing trip would be. And it wasn't so much about the fishing as it was about getting back to his family origins. He was really looking forward to spending time with his dad and brothers, he told me many times. I picture Rachel handing him a beer.

And at the time I figured he might be cracking his beer open, I was chucking my empties into the trash. It had been a good day for me: fishing, talking, and reminiscing. It sounded exactly like what we hoped to do when four men in four different states would come together in the same place, a reuniting of the family that I was born into, but left when I started a family of my own.

"Honey? It's me," I said to Jean over the phone. "How are you doing? How are the girls?"

"We're good, just getting dinner ready. We're going to eat in about an hour. Stop by the store and get some milk please," she said.

I kicked back for a little while, letting whatever minimal buzz I had wear off. With my feet on the wooden folding chair, I revisited what Rabbi Kushner told me months earlier about the lack of male bonding in the world and how that leaves a good many of us "emotionally impoverished." How true.

I hoped this trip would enrich us as a family, making us better brothers, sons, fathers, and, if at all possible, friends. That of course involved a *choice*. We had no choice about the blood that flows through our veins, and the family name that outsiders use to paint us as one, but we *can* choose our friends.

On the way home from the trout pond I swung by Roche Brothers in Wellesley and grabbed a gallon of milk. When I walked into my home, I was greeted by daughters Sammy and Amanda, my German Shepherd Beverly, and my wife, Jean. A pleasant smell of chicken soup wafted from the kitchen, which, as smells often do, brought back warm memories of my childhood. Back then my brothers and I would bum rush my dad at the door, followed by our mom and our Cairn Terrier Danielle.

Now I'm that guy coming home to the hugging and mugging of girls, a big dog instead of a small one, and the mom is my wife. My, oh my, how my life has changed. I am blessed, and I wonder where the time has gone.

TWO

Meet My Dad, Bob

Bob Walsh tying flies, Ledyard, Conn., 2012

My dad is a Jersey boy and proud of it. He's also a twin. During his delivery the doctor called out, "There's one more!"

That was my Uncle Dick. My dad and my uncle were the best of friends. There's a lesson in that. For them it came easily, but that doesn't mean their lives were easy. World War II began a month before Dad and Dick were born in 1939. The war and illness greatly shaped Dad's life and the life of his family.

Japan's attack on Pearl Harbor on December 7, 1941, was a tipping point. Dad's dad, my grandfather, went off to serve. That broke up the family temporarily. The twins and their older brother and sister went to live with their maternal grandparents in Providence, Rhode Island. The twins were so young they hardly understood the turmoil around them. Plus they always had each other. That was until 1945.

Uncle Dick hadn't been feeling well for weeks. Doctors thought he might have Cat Scratch Fever. It was far worse. On August 15, Victory Over Japan Day, Dad's best friend was diagnosed with polio. Uncle Dick went to Warm Springs, Georgia, for treatment for a year. With his parents shuttling back and forth between the Northeast and the South, my dad was sent to live with his paternal grandparents in the Jamaica Plain section of Boston.

Dad missed his twin brother terribly, but he had plenty of cousins to play with across the street. By the time Dick was well enough to come back North, Dad was back from Boston and with his family in Montclair, New Jersey. When Dick came hobbling into the house on Essex Avenue, Dad wasn't prepared for what he saw or heard. The polio had severely damaged Dick's legs. The leg braces were heavy and went clackety clack. And when Dick spoke, it was clear he had picked up a Southern drawl.

Dad was thrilled to have his brother and best friend back. They had to make some adjustments in their play, so they did. They rode bikes together, played catch, danced, and fought. As we know, kids can be cruel. Dad had no tolerance for those who taunted his twin brother. One time an older neighborhood kid called Dick a cripple. Dad and another friend chased the insensitive jerk down, dragged him back, and watched Dick all but squeeze the life out of the bully.

More than anything, Dad loved to fish. Sometimes he fished with Dick at a pond down the street. Other times he fished with friends and an adult neighbor. Quite often he fished alone. He had no problem with that and his parents never worried about him. He liked the solitude.

Like just about every other American kid, Dad played sandlot baseball. He was decent, but he couldn't hit. His older brother, Al, taught him how to bat left handed. That helped, but just a smidge. Dad's high school yearbook says he swam a wicked butterfly and played halfback on the football team. I asked him about the football and he admitted he didn't get a lot of touches. He said he was slow. It was an unfortunate gene that he would pass along.

Dad went to Georgetown and was in the ROTC program. He served in the Air Force after graduation. After finishing up his military commitment, he briefly worked in the telephone industry in New York City. It wasn't his thing. Eventually he hung up on that. He married my mom and found his career calling in research and development. He's a good man and was a good husband to a good lady who's no longer with us.

Dad is on his second marriage. No one in the world is enjoying love and life the second time around more than he. The happiness that lives within him is a reward for a life well lived—a life that includes immeasurable heartbreak, resiliency, honor, honesty, example, and good citizenship. He's quite active for a man his age despite some health setbacks in his fifties. He had a couple of strokes twenty years ago that left him with a slight limp, which has worsened over the years. But by and large he's pretty darned healthy. His speech is clear and his mind sharp.

When he's not fishing, or building fly rods for someone he knows, my dad is feeding the homeless at area shelters. He gives back because he knows life has been good to him.

THREE

Coming Home

Kevin, Bob, Michael, and Christopher Walsh, Ledyard, Conn., November 2012

The journey among family men was just about here. It was Saturday, November 17, the night before the Sunday morning launch from Dad's house in Connecticut. It was a little after 11, and I was sitting at my desk at Comcast SportsNet in Burlington, Mass., watching unbelievable drama on my desktop flat screen TV.

Stanford sophomore kicker Jordan Williamson lined up a 37-yard field goal attempt in overtime against Oregon. If he made it, the thirteenth-ranked Cardinal would win. That would keep the number two Ducks from ascending to number one in the nation after the top-ranked Kansas State Wildcats were upset by Baylor earlier in the day.

It had been a tough night for the highly touted kicker out of Austin, Texas. He missed a 43-yarder earlier in the third quarter and was just 12 for 20 on field goal attempts for the season. Tied at 14 and with the pressure mounting inside the hostile Autzen Stadium, Williamson gave his holder Daniel Zychlinski a gentle nod. Zychlinski lifted his right hand and called for the ball. Long snapper Jacob Gowan fired a strike between his legs and into the hands of Zychlinski who caught it cleanly, put it down, spun the laces, and gave the ball a little tilt.

Williamson took two steps toward the ball, cocked his right leg back, and buggy whipped it through the hold. The ball started down the left third of the uprights with a gentle draw. It snuck inside the left goalpost by about two feet. The Stanford sideline erupted. Williamson took off running down the field to avoid teammates who wanted to pile on top of him. He eventually ended up in the arms of freshman quarterback Kevin Hogan.

In Palo Alto, Stanford students leaped into each other's arms and fountain hopped around campus. The win was redemption and retribution. Stanford's only regular season losses in 2010 and 2011 were to Oregon. The thrilling win also turned the BCS bowl and national championship picture upside down for the second straight week. The upsets of the top two teams in America lifted number three Notre Dame to the top of the polls for the first time in nineteen years.

It was just a few minutes after I finished anchoring the 10:30 edition of SportsNet Central, a sports highlights show that caters to New England fans who just can't get enough of sports. Comcast SportsNet is an all sports network, reaching four million homes in six states. The ten or so staff members left on this night—producers, editors, and directors—watched the same game and we all whooped and hollered. This is why we do what we do.

Earlier we watched the Celtics clobber the Toronto Raptors on our air in a rare Saturday afternoon game at the TD Garden. We had reports from Gillette Stadium in Foxborough where the Patriots were preparing to host Sunday's game against the Indianapolis Colts. Most days are really good at work, but this day was exceptional.

Barring any late breaking news that would require a redo of the 10:30 SportsNet Central show, it would hold for the morning repeats. Still, we couldn't leave until just before midnight. That gave us time to catch up on the games that we couldn't watch on TV because we were on TV. Watching a game is usually a great way to unwind, but sometimes we get wound up even more. Jordan Williamson's game-winning field goal sent a buzz through the building.

About a hundred miles south, Michael Walsh had a pretty good buzz going too. He was at a bachelor party at David's Cafe in Preston, Conn. After a long week of work and a difficult day of travel from Atlanta with two small children who had never flown before, he could have used a couple of beers. Now that he was among his high school friends, he didn't have to be anyone other than himself. There was no rushing, no hushing, no fussing, and no diaper changes. That was a change from how the day started.

Michael shared his story with me later.

Tired from a late night of doing laundry and unpacking, Mike had gotten up early Saturday morning to take the dog to the kennel. From there he swung by the in-laws to pick up Lolo. Lolo is what Mike's children call their grandfather—Mike's father-in-law, John Morgan. Lolo rode with the family to the airport and drove the car home. Four-year-old Anne was excited to see Lolo, and she absolutely could not wait to ride the plane and see her older cousins in New England. Peter is just a year and a half old so he didn't really know what was up.

There was a problem. Mike's wife Rachel couldn't find her cell phone.

Mike told me he turned the car around and headed back to Sandy Springs, north of the city. He pulled in the driveway and Rachel ran inside. Mike called Rachel's number, hoping she would hear the phone ring and follow her ears. There was a buzzing sound in the back of the car. It was Rachel's phone on vibrate. It was packed away in a travel bag. So they found the phone, but they lost time. Mike began to wonder what other trouble might lie ahead.

The airport drop-off presented its own challenges. The departures curbside was crowded, which meant it was dangerous. There were two child seats to undo from the car and four bags to unload from the trunk. Managing two toddlers who could easily wander off made a tough thing nearly impossible. Mike just wanted to get on that plane and buckle the kids in.

Once they boarded the plane, Mike and Rachel divided the labor. He took Peter, Rachel focused on Anne. Peter started making faces while fussing in his seat. It was that unmistakable look followed by that unmistakable smell. Peter had pooped his pants. It was the last minute before the plane started taxiing away from the terminal, and the flight crew wanted everyone to stay put.

Mike put Peter under his arm and dashed for the lavatory. There was no changing table inside. This had to be a stand-up change. Oh it was a bad one. Mike left the steaming diaper in the toilet and headed back to his seat with Peter tucked under his arm. There was a nasty exchange going on between a female flight attendant and a well-to-do passenger. The passenger didn't appreciate the crew member's pushiness in telling him to secure his bag in the overhead space and to get seated quickly. The only good thing about the heated exchange was the cover it provided for the diaper duty duck-out.

The two hour and forty minute flight to Boston was largely uneventful, with the exception of Anne taking peeks out the window like any child on her first flight would. As the plane descended toward Logan International Airport, Mike enjoyed the view of the skyline and thought about all the good times he had in the city as a student at Boston College. He could hardly believe it had been thirteen years since he graduated, and four years since he'd been back to New England.

He looked over at Rachel and smiled. Boston has been good to her too. It's where they met and lived for a couple of years after college. They were not only going back to the region where Mike has deep family roots, they were also retracing the steps where the roots of their family together were sown.

After securing a rental car for Rachel and the children, Michael sent them on their way to Sturbridge, Massachusetts, where they would stay with old friends for a couple of days. Michael hopped on a train bound for Mystic, Connecticut. The hour-and-a-half train ride south took him back in time. The coach attendants had New England accents as thick as *chowda*. It had been a while since

Mike had been on a train, because it's not a primary means of travel in the South like it is in the Northeast.

Inside the cafe car Mike spotted a boy who looked to be about twelve years old and was traveling alone. The crew members kept coming back to check up on him. It reminded Mike of all the times he used to ride the Amtrak between Connecticut and Philadelphia when he was that age. The difference was, back then, nobody checked up on him. Mike loved the motion and sound of the train, the view outside the window, and the independence of traveling alone. He still loves the train.

When the Amtrak rolled into Mystic, the father of the groom was waiting to pick him up. He took Mike home where a party bus waited to take all the boys to a catered dinner at the firehouse, followed by a night at the bar. Figuring it would be a late night for Mike, and presuming that I'd be driving through the town of Preston around 2 a.m. after my work shift was over, we planned for me to be Mike's ride home to Dad's house in Ledyard. It was convenient, and it ensured that my little brother would have a sober ride home. He could party to his heart's content until I got there, just like the kids at Stanford would likely be doing hours after the big win over Oregon.

I was eager to catch up with my little brother, but I was still at work. Following Jordan Williamson's game-winning field goal, I was flying a holding pattern at my desk. I read all the major sports websites trying to cram knowledge into my head, knowing that I'd be going into an information black hole for a couple of days. Just before midnight I got the okay to leave work.

I stopped at home in Wellesley briefly to change out of my suit and into more comfortable sweats for the ninety-minute ride to Connecticut. I took my German Shepherd Beverly out for a late night potty break and chucked my fishing gear and luggage into the covered bed of my truck. I went back inside, kissed my stirring wife, Jean, goodbye, and opened the door of my girls' room and blew kisses from the door.

About forty-five minutes into the ride south, I got a text message from Mike. He didn't need a ride after all. Dad and another interested family member picked him up at the bar a bit early.

Chris Walsh was riding shotgun in the front seat of Dad's Forrester, sharing stories about an interesting day of travel for him too. Chris had arrived at San Antonio International Airport at 6:15 a.m. for a 7:15 flight. There was already a line out the door. Because he was flying Southwest, there were no assigned seats. He was worried that he might get stuck in a middle seat. He dodged the booby seat, but he couldn't dodge the sight of a little boy in the terminal picking his nose and eating boogies. It reminded him of Spalding doing the same in the movie *Caddyshack*.

It got better. And he eagerly related these travel events when he saw me. The plane he flew in was painted to resemble Shamu. The lead flight attendant had a whale of a time on the plane's PA system, delivering the flight instructions with the kind of pizzazz one might expect from a human or animal performer at SeaWorld. The trouble was, it was hard to understand him. He had a bad lisp and the cabin had bad acoustics.

"Are you getting this?" Chris asked the woman across the aisle.

"No," she answered, "but he's sure having fun with that microphone."

After takeoff, and once the flying whale reached a comfortable cruising altitude, Chris settled into his aisle seat. He thought about our family and where we grew up, never imagining how much the vagaries of life, education, opportunity, and necessity would move us all in different directions.

Then he advanced the thinking to what was waiting on the other end: the reunion of brothers at the direction of the man who taught them all how to fish. It was a good reflection until another passenger interrupted him. The woman sitting next to him in the center row got up some five times to retrieve items from the overhead bin. That meant Chris had to get up so she could get around him time and time again.

A couple of rows up, a loudmouth was bragging to anyone within earshot that he spent $150,000 dollars at the Mercedes dealership. If that was true, why would such a big fish be flying a discount airline with loud colors and whales painted on its planes? What a loser. If nothing else, what was annoying to Chris in the air turned out to be good storytelling on the ground.

"That's really funny," Dad said.

This was Dad's second taxi run of the day having picked Chris up at Bradley International Airport in Hartford in the afternoon. Chris ran into David's Cafe, fetched Mike, and pretty soon they were rolling into the driveway at the family homestead in Ledyard.

Jacked up on adrenaline, coffee, and a mouthful of Frito Lay ranch-flavored sunflower seeds, I trucked down I-395. I didn't feel tired at all, even though I had been up for twenty straight hours. Based on my estimated 2:45 a.m. arrival time, and Dad's desire to get up at 7:30, I'd be lucky to get a little more than four hours of shuteye. That wouldn't be so bad if I didn't have to drive another seven and a half hours to Western New York on short sleep, but we'd worry about that later.

It was the deer rut season and there were other things to worry about first. There were carcasses off to the side of 395 and along highway 164. I've come close to collisions with deer in these parts before, and it didn't help that there were quite a few cars on the narrow highway that meanders through the cornfields and forest of Jewett City and Preston. Considering the late hour, I guessed many of the other drivers were under the influence of something other than seeds and caffeinated beverages.

Fortunately no deer jumped in front of my truck, and the other drivers stayed on their side of the yellow line. Just before 3 a.m. I rolled into my dad's driveway, ran up the stairs to the blue guest bedroom, and crashed within seconds of my head hitting the pillow.

FOUR

Meet My Older Brother, Chris

Family dinner, Ledyard, Conn., November 2012. Left to right: Kevin Walsh, Rachel Walsh holding Peter Walsh, Victor Zhang, Mary McGrattan, Bob Walsh, and Chris Walsh, the photo bomber

Have a look at the photo bomber. How can you possibly take that man seriously? Let me tell you something. Looks are deceiving. My brother Chris is about as serious as a call from the IRS. This is no secret to us, or anyone who knows my forty-four-year-old brother. What's at the core of it? Being the oldest sibling. And his similarities to our late mother are good places to start.

Not only does my brother bear a striking resemblance to our mom, he acts like her in so many ways. Mom was the first born in a family of two girls. She took her role as big sister very seriously. Chris carries the same obligation as the big brother. Nobody told him he had to do it, he took it upon himself. If he were a dog he'd be a German Shepherd. He's big, strong, intensely loyal, and always on guard even if there's nothing to be on guard for. And like most German Shepherds, or at least the ones I've raised, there's a softer side to the grizzled exterior.

Chris was athletic with a good set of hands. His eye-hand coordination made him a great hitter in Abington/Roychester Little League baseball in Abington, Pennsylvania. But his cement wheels left him parked behind the plate as catcher. It's not his fault that he was slow then, and still is. It's hereditary. Chris insists he's faster than I am, but I'm not so sure. A race would have settled it, but there was never a rush to make it happen. We both would have lost.

Chris was really into dogs from the time we were young. We have pictures of him as an infant climbing on top of a massive St. Bernard named Murphy. Murphy was our first family dog. He loved Chris and Chris loved Murphy. They would play together wonderfully, and Chris had no fear touching Murphy's teeth and eyeballs with his baby fingers. But later Murphy developed serious behavior issues. To put it bluntly, he went crazy. He ferociously bit my dad and his friend. With such a small child and another child on the way (me), Murphy had to be put down.

Chris more or less adopted the neighbors' dogs as his own. He had no problem going over to the Reutemanns and asking, "Can I borrow your dog for the day?" Susie, the copper-colored Labrador mix practically lived with us for a couple of years before we bought a new family pet. Everybody we knew had a dog back in the early 1970s and Chris was sort of a Dog Whisperer before anyone knew the term or knew who noted dog trainer Cesar Millan was. Tarzan was the King of the Jungle, and the man about animals back then. We called Chris Tarzan. He quite liked it.

As we got older, Chris kept his pigeon-toed feet in sports, but he was really into working. He had an assortment of odd jobs that most teenagers did in the 1980s. He started caddying at Huntingdon Valley Country Club. The thing with caddying is, it's either in you or it's not. It wasn't in him.

He later worked as the cleaning boy at a local gym and at Wilburger's ski shop. He really enjoyed the ski shop and the employee discount. He bought a lot of good equipment and put it to good use on the slopes of the Pocono Mountains in Northeastern Pennsylvania.

Despite a heavy load of schoolwork, high school lacrosse and working at Wilburger's, he managed a robust social life too. He and his friends were really into music—The Who and U2, especially. Because he worked, Chris always had enough money to buy cool stuff including the first Sony Walkman and all its subsequent versions. He gave me his castoff cassette players, but he laughed at me for playing Hall and Oates in them.

As an older brother, Chris broke in our parents. He wasn't a bad kid in any way, but he did plenty of normal high school stuff that makes most parents nibble their nails down to nubs. He had parties, went to parties, and on occasion came home late from parties. But there was never any reason to suspect it was anything other than a phase.

Chris got good grades, scored well on the SAT, and went to college at Villanova University where he received a degree in commerce and finance. He's living the life just about everybody thought he would. The fact that he's married, has three kids, a couple of dogs and works in the finance industry is a surprise to no one. This is what we all thought he'd be doing. That sounds like something you'd smile about. But like I said, Chris is about as serious as a tax audit.

FIVE

Four Guys Four Wheelin'

Starting from left clockwise: Chris Walsh with exchange student Victor Zhang, Michael Walsh, Bob Walsh, and Mary McGrattan, Ledyard, Conn., 2012

Kevin and Bob Walsh, Ledyard, Conn., November 2012

A shift in the family dynamic was coming. Dad had no clue. It was just as well. He might have resisted if he knew what was up. Here's the deal, we didn't know it was about to happen either. That wouldn't make it any less important. It would happen naturally, which I think was best. It would be honest. But it would only happen outside the walls of Dad's house when the seven-and-a-half-hour, 500-mile drive to the fishing grounds in Fredonia, New York, began. Inside it's still Dad's world.

"Kevin! Time to get up! Let's go, it's time to get UP!"

If you ever needed an example of how Dad's military roots never left him, being awakened by him is among the best examples. There's an absolute charge in his voice. Don't bother asking for another five minutes because you're not getting it. It's best just to get up. I heard quick knock-knocks on the other doors down the hall followed by, "Chris, Michael ..." followed by the same speech I just got.

It was 7:30 as I swung my legs out from under the sheets and wool blanket and onto the soft carpet. I sat on the side of the bed and rubbed the sleep out of my eyes. I saw my travel bag all packed and ready to go. I never opened it when I had arrived just a couple of hours earlier. There was no need to change my clothes because I slept in the same ones I'd wear for the long drive ahead. No shower, we're men. We would rough it! A quick rub of Speed Stick under the arms did just fine.

The one thing I wouldn't do without—breakfast. I was starving and badly in need of my first cup of coffee of the day.

Downstairs in the center of the kitchen table was a bowl filled with bananas, apples, pears, and grapes. Our stepmother Mary was making quiche with home fried potatoes and muffins. Sitting at the table was the newest addition to our family. Sixteen-year-old Victor is a foreign exchange student from China. Victor immediately got up, smiled, and extended his hand for a shake. He's very personable and respectful. His English isn't perfect, but it's good. Victor attends Ledyard High and rides the school bus just like everybody else.

Over breakfast Victor told me about his family and where he's from. He lives in Qingdao, a bustling city of 11 million people on the southeastern coast of mainland China. Despite China's being the most populous nation on earth, Victor is the product of the "new" China where families are limited to having one child. He has no siblings and now he was surrounded by them with his "new" family. Life in sleepy, bucolic Connecticut couldn't be much more different than Qingdao. Still, he's thriving in the home-away-from-home experience, and he was exceptionally curious about the life we Walsh brothers lived growing up.

After breakfast we headed outside to load up my truck. Victor and Mary came out to take pictures and to see us on our way. Dad wanted a specific picture of all the fishermen holding the fly rods he built especially for us, which were inside hand-sewn pouches that Mary made for the trip. As we posed on the back of my tailgate, Victor snapped away. After a dozen or so pictures, it was time to roll.

Dad wanted to drive, but it wasn't his choice. It's my truck, so I would drive. There was no tension and there wasn't really a power struggle, but there was a changing of the guard. Dad was always the driver wherever we went. Not this time. He moved over to the front passenger seat, ceding the power of seniority that he's had as long as we've known him.

He didn't have control of the wheel, but Dad was determined to have some control by not giving me the driving directions that I asked for.

"Just follow the GPS," he said firmly as we pulled out of the driveway.

"All right, everyone, listen up," I announced. "I want to lay down some ground rules."

"No, no ground rules," Dad shot back.

"Wait a minute. It's my truck. I make the rules."

Dad looked really annoyed, but he backed off.

"There will be no farting, no spilling of dip, no ..."

Dad realized I was joking, but I had him going for a second.

Chris sat directly behind me and Michael was next to him. I have an extended cab in my truck, but those were two large men filling up the space. Chris is 6 feet 3 inches, 230 pounds, with dark brown eyes and matching hair. He has as much hair as he did when he was twenty-four, and the color has hardly changed. I'm suspicious of that.

Mike is a little taller and probably thirty pounds lighter than Chris. At thirty-five he's the same age as New England Patriots quarterback Tom Brady and actually kind of looks like him. Mike has Brady's round face, same colored hair, and the quarterback's Jesse "The Body" Ventura–like dimple and cleft chin. When you see us brothers together, you know we're siblings. There's just enough "Walsh" in our faces, but not enough to say, "Oh yeah, they're clones."

The most obvious difference between my brothers and me is height. I'm 5 feet 9 inches, and my brothers are not above making fun of me to cut me down. One time during a family wedding some twenty years ago, we were trying to get set for a picture of the brothers. Mike and Chris went down the old, tired road.

"Kev, why are you so short? Let's get a box for him to stand on."

Chris's mother-in-law, Jewel Finaldi, was holding the camera and rather enjoying the good-natured brotherly kidding. She joined in. "They got all the height, but you got all the looks!"

"*Yes!* I like that," I said as I took the center spot and wrapped my arms around Chris and Mike.

The blood left Chris's face. *"Thanks a lot, Jewel,"* Chris said knowing he'd been had.

Now I don't know if I'm more handsome than Chris and Mike, but when they tease me about my height, I play the Jewel card and we immediately go back to that moment in time at the wedding. It drives my brothers crazy, which is exactly the point.

The long drive to the tributaries of Lake Erie brought back a lot of memories. The last time we were together in a vehicle for that long was more than thirty years ago when we used to drive from suburban Philadelphia to visit my grandmother in Wakefield, Rhode Island. My brothers and I brawled and bawled the entire time. Dad kept one hand on the steering wheel and reached into the backseat with the other while trying to break things up.

If those childhood rides weren't so bad, our memories of them wouldn't be so good. And even though we had a long way to go here, the time in the truck would fly as simple glances, conversations, and other visuals would take us back in time, place, and spirit to where our journey as a fishing band of men began.

No sooner had we left Dad's neighborhood, Mike and Chris turned the backseat into a mobile office. Mike was on a deadline with a new job that he earned after his ninety-day contract. A report was due before the end of the day. Like a lot of folks who take vacation around the holidays, it often means a crush of work in the days before. Mike crunched his laptop keyboard with fast, heavy typing. He knew he'd get the work done, but he had to hustle.

Were he my friend, I might have glibly told him to lighten up a bit. But he's my brother. The stakes are higher. I found myself in the uncomfortable juxtaposition of wanting to ease his pain, but knowing he might just have to slog through it alone without the brotherly commentary. I said nothing.

Dad stole looks in the truck's side mirror. He wished his youngest son could just use the ride to unwind, but he understood that Michael is the new guy at the office who needs to impress and prove he's reliable. I sneaked peeks in the rearview mirror too, angling the mirror and getting a better look at Mike than Dad could from his seat.

Mike picked up on it and acknowledged, "I have a hard time putting things out of my mind and have trouble relaxing when I owe people work."

Chris checked his iPhone for email. There were quite a few already on a Sunday morning. It was hard to tell whether he was annoyed because my older brother often looks annoyed even when he's not. Like the German Shepherd I compared Chris to, now that I think about it, he also wears the perpetual look of a man who returned to his car to find a parking ticket on it. He is so serious.

Maybe I should have told my older brother to just chill out. Not just now, but with life in general. I wanted to, but I was sure he didn't want to hear it—especially from me. *Shut up,* I could hear him say in my mind's ear. That gave me pause. Were we not brothers I would have said plenty. Instead, I was silent. That's twice if you were counting.

Whatever messages Chris received on his iPhone, I got the feeling the replies could wait. He wasn't typing, just scrolling. I looked over at Dad and he was fidgeting. Dad said so much by saying nothing. He's relieved that his days in this working world are done.

SIX

Meet My Younger Brother, Michael

Michael Walsh (right) with childhood friend Christopher McGrath, 1984

When I think of my younger brother, Michael, I sometimes think about our mother. It has nothing to do with his looks. Mike looks more like our dad than he does our mom. I remember her being pregnant and my having a hard time wrapping my head around the fact that we were about to have another brother.

Check that, we didn't know it was going to be a boy. In fact, I remember my dad thinking it was going to be a girl. I don't know why he felt that way. The odds are fifty-fifty each time and completely independent of previous results. Plus there was no ultrasound in 1977. Even if there was, Dad says they didn't want to know what they were getting until it came out.

And so it was, early on a summer morning, the child that Dad was ready to call Susie turned out to be Michael. Seven years younger than I, and nine years younger than Chris, Mike almost seemed to be of a different generation. He played team sports: Little League baseball, lacrosse, and basketball. He wasn't as athletic or intense as Chris and I, but he could play well enough, and he never lost sight of the fact that sports were supposed to be fun.

Mike also enjoyed building super-fast remote-controlled cars with our dad. Those model cars were exceptionally detailed and took hours to put together. Mike would wait for cars to drive by our house and then chase them with the car he built.

When I think of funny Mike moments, I remember him playing tennis. It wasn't about serve and volley, it was about who was on the other side of the net. Mike always seemed to be playing with pretty girls who were much older than he. One day I saw him walking away from the tennis courts at a nearby club where our family had a membership. He had on somebody else's sneakers.

I asked, "Whose sneakers are you wearing?"

"Oh, they're Yvonne's," he answered like it wasn't anything at all.

Hold on. There's something you need to know here. Yvonne is not her real name, but it sure sounds like it. Yvonne was nine years older than Mike and the prettiest, kindest girl you could ever imagine. There was not a boy about her age who didn't have a crush on her. Yvonne treated Michael like a little brother. To see this seventeen-year-old All-American girl patiently hitting ground strokes with my eight-year-old brother was really something. Mike knew the reaction the dynamic brought and he played it off as Joe Cool. It was cool and it was innocent, even if he can't remember all the details.

"I never wore Yvonne's sneakers," Mike protests. "That's gross wearing someone else's shoes. But you're right, I did play tennis with a lot of older girls."

Mike's memory is as challenged as his eyesight. He had poor eyesight at a very young age. One time during summer vacation he came back to our rental house in Ocean City, New Jersey, distraught about having lost his glasses in the ocean.

"Wait, you wore your glasses while you were surfing?" I asked Mike incredulously.

"Yeah," he answered.

"And you didn't think something like that would happen after a wipeout or duck dive?" I asked with a laugh.

"Well, I thought the cables around my ears would keep them on."

The rest of that vacation was pretty fuzzy for Mike because he's practically blind without his specs. The abuse I gave him over the glasses gaffe was just a small sample of the larger body of ribbing work I subjected him to throughout much of our childhood. Even if Mike was a little absent minded about such things as surfing with prescription glasses on, he's brilliant with just about everything else. He's a heckuva lot smarter than I am, and I'm sure Chris would concede that Mike is smarter than he is too.

Mike did well to go to Boston College, and even better when he put himself through the MBA program at University of North Carolina. But the best thing he ever did was marry

Rachel Morgan. He's worked in the computer industry, finance, research, and consulting. He's done a lot, and I'm proud of him. How he did that, minus the woman who brought him into the world, God only knows.

SEVEN

It'll Be Better Fishing Where We're Going

As we worked our way across the Mohegan–Pequot Bridge on CT 2A West, there was a sizable bank of fog settled in over the Thames River below. Dad and I used to fish the Thames at night when I was in my early twenties. We would cross the train tracks farther down in the direction of the Long Island Sound and cast heavily weighted lines with blood worms on hooks into the darkness.

I never caught a thing in the Thames, but that wasn't so much the point. It was time together with Dad during a period in his life when he was lonely and grieving Mom's death. I looked over at Dad and he was looking down at the river too.

"We never really had much luck down there," I told him.

He looked over and smiled with a gleam in his eye, "It'll be a lot better where we're going."

Chris heard the comment and looked up from his iPhone. I caught his reflection in the rearview mirror and our eyes locked for just about a second. That's not a lot of time on a clock, but for guys—especially brothers—it's an eternity. Every time I see my brother's face, I see my mother. It's impossible not to. They look so much alike. Does he see it too? I've asked him before.

"Definitely. The moles, the cheeks, the eyes, the hair and its texture. I even see it in my kids now," he says somberly.

I saw Michael in the mirror too. He knew there was something wrong with Mom before the rest of us did. He found her on the floor in the kitchen after hearing an awful crash. He was just eight years old at the time. And as I turned my eyes back to the road I thought he had to grow up too fast.

About a mile past the bridge and off to the right rose the spectacular Mohegan Sun Casino. The rising morning sun set off a bedazzling reflection on the side of the casino's glassy exterior, perfectly matching the casino name and its famous TV commercial in which the announcer says at the end, "When it's your time to shine come see us."

But there's another voice track in the middle of that same spot that spoke more directly to the men riding inside my truck. "What's that great old saying about strangers? They're just friends you haven't met yet." Okay maybe the collective group in my truck wasn't the young sexy crowd the ad is designed for, and we weren't strangers, but I was hoping this trip would make us better friends. We'd see about that. We were only about twenty minutes into it.

Just as I heard the Mohegan Sun spot play in my head, the real voice of the GPS lady filled my ears with instructions, "In a quarter mile, take the exit right to 395 North."

It was a short four miles on 395 North before we exited on Highway 2 West, bound for Hartford, about fifty minutes away. Approaching Hartford, the state capital, we merged onto 84 West before taking 91 North, across the Massachusetts state line and into Springfield, home of the Basketball Hall of Fame.

We were hoping to make it another twenty minutes and reach I-90 West before stopping for gas, but my bladder balked so we pulled over in West Springfield. This is driver's privilege. Nobody complained because they too had been holding it in for a while. Mike finished typing a sentence, put his computer aside, and climbed out with the rest of us.

We all used the bathroom, then headed for the convenience store. I stocked up on sunflower seeds, Chris got some chew, and Michael gathered an assortment of snacks and sodas. Dad offered cash, but nobody took it.

When it came time to fill up the gas tank outside, Dad insisted on paying for that too. "Dad, don't worry about it. I got it," I told him.

"No, no. I want to pay," he protested, slowly hobbling around the truck waving his credit card.

I waved him off. I had already slid my card into the slot and activated the pump. He shook his head knowing that he was a step too slow. Slowly but surely, more changes of the guard were happening all around him. We helped him climb back into the truck because his legs just don't have the lift they once did. For so long he took care of us. Now we're slowly transitioning to the phase of life where we take care of him. He's a proud man, but not so modest that he won't accept help from the sons who are proud that he's their dad.

The drive so far took us as much north as it did west. In Chicopee, Massachusetts, we merged onto 90 West. An hour later we crossed the New York State line by Canaan. We were two hours and thirty minutes into the trip, with five more to go. I-90 brought us past Albany, Schenectady, and two and a half hours after crossing the state line, we rolled past Syracuse. Mike was rolling on his report. Didn't hear much from him in the five hours of driving.

From Syracuse on, the final couple of hours of the drive to Fredonia would be almost straight west, with a little drop to the south once we reached Buffalo. Fifty minutes past Syracuse we passed the Finger Lakes region.

"Dad, why do they call it the Finger Lakes region?" I asked.

"It's because there are a series of lakes and they look like fingers on a hand," he answered.

"Think the fishing's any good there?" I followed up.

"Oh, I guess so, but it'll ...," he started.

"Yeah, yeah, yeah, Dad, I think I got it," interrupting. "It'll be a lot better where we're going," stealing his now famous line.

I looked up at Chris in the rearview mirror and he was shaking his head like it was the most unoriginal thing to say, which was exactly the point.

"Whaddaya got against the Finger Lakes?" I asked with a laugh.

"Nothing," he answered while giving me the finger with a laugh of his own.

A half hour after Chris flipped me the bird, we passed the exit for Rochester. We were now 380 miles into the trip with about 120 miles to go. Mike was full steam ahead on that report, and Chris just launched a godawful fart that was exacerbated by his dipping.

"You might want to check your drawers after that one," I said while rolling down the windows just as he opened his Skoal mint tin for another pinch of chew.

The blast of cold Western New York wind not only cleared the foul air, it also blew a layer off the top of the tobacco and onto Chris's clothes.

"Ahhh," he screamed as the fine cut made a fine mess of his pants. Nothing better.

Shortly after Chris made a mess of the outside, and possibly the inside of his pants, Dad's phone rang.

"Hi, Paul," Dad said.

Paul was our guide from Reel Action Fly Fishing. He wanted to know where we were.

"We're coming up on Batavia," Dad told him.

"Get off at Batavia," Paul said, "find a place to stay, and I'll see you at 4:15 tomorrow morning."

It was a good thing Paul called when he did. The Batavia exit was upon us just seconds later. There was a change of plans. The fishing had been better around Lake Ontario than Lake Erie at the time, so we'd fish the former's tributaries instead. That saved us another 90 miles of driving too. Perfect! We were tired, hungry, and thirsty after more than 400 miles of driving and a couple of stops.

EIGHT

Brothers Fight Over Beer—in Walmart

We saw a cluster of hotels and motels near Batavia Downs—a horse-racing track and casino. Dad wanted the Comfort Inn, which is the same chain we had reservations with in Fredonia, New York, before Paul told us to detour. But Michael, a frequent traveler, made a wise overrule. He insisted we'd be better off at the Holiday Inn Express where the rooms are bigger with more amenities.

Holiday Inn Express cost a little more than the Comfort Inn, but we justified the added expense by using Mike's reward points to upgrade to suites. Mike is a modest man, but he won't skimp on accommodations. His life on the road is a constant reminder that you get what you pay for. Don't sleep cheap. You won't sleep well. Dad? Well, he could sleep inside a box.

Normally Dad would handle the check in, but not this time. Michael did it all at the front desk, sparing Dad the effort. He returned with four sets of card keys: room 208 for Chris and him, 106 for Dad and me. We unloaded the truck and brought the luggage inside on a faux brassy bellhop cart. Dad didn't have to touch a thing. We took care of his stuff for him.

Once we unpacked inside our rooms, we drove to Walmart to buy fishing licenses. There were Girl Scouts with their mothers selling cookies out front. I bought a box of Thin Mints. My daughters, Samantha and Amanda, are Girl Scouts. They've spent many a cold day with Mom outside our neighborhood grocery store doing the same thing. There was no way I could say no.

Inside Walmart, a man named Joe was working the register in sporting goods. He typed all of our personal information into a computer with one hand instead of two. That wouldn't have been so bad were he not so slow. It took almost a half hour. My brothers and I were getting impatient. Dad hardly seemed to care. This was one of those "small stuff" things that he doesn't sweat anymore, but it drove his sons crazy.

Armed with licenses and legal to fish, Dad went outside for a smoke, and we three headed over to the food section of the superstore. There was no issue over the snacks and microwavable breakfast foods we selected for purchase, but there was a righteous debate in the beer aisle over brands, bottles, and cans.

I wanted a local microbrew. I think that's part of the fun of being in a new place—drinking what the locals do.

"My appreciation for microbrews has come and gone," Michael said dismissingly. "When I'm this close to the border, I want Canadian beer. Labatt preferably, and in cans. It's a fishing trip for Chrissakes!"

Well excuuuse me. Chris is a can guy too. I prefer bottles.

"Whaddaya some kinda beer snob, Kev?" Chris asked sarcastically.

"Well, why would you ever want the taste of metal in your beer? It corrupts the flavor," was my response.

"No, it adds to the flavor," Chris argued.

"Yeah. It makes it worse," I countered.

We compromised. We got a case of Labatt Blue cans and a Labatt bottles sampler pack with different colored ales, Marzen and Classic Porter. We took the loot back to the hotel, put the beer on ice, took showers, and Mike put the finishing touches on his research report before emailing it to the office.

We ordered pizza, washed it down with a couple of cold ones, and called it a night early. At least some of us did.

NINE
On Fish, Fish On!

Michael Walsh, Western New York, 2012

I thought a war was breaking out when the alarm shook the room at 3:45 a.m. The alarm clock was programmed to sound like an air raid siren. How obnoxious, and how effective. No way anyone could sleep through that. Dad was up fast. He was scurrying around the room in his skivvies with a zest younger than his years. He was so jacked up, so early in the morning.

"Make sure you call your brothers upstairs to make sure they're up too," he instructed before ducking into the shower.

Turns out Mike and Chris didn't need to be roused from bed. They were up and moving along at a reasonable pace. I opted not to shower, instead dressing quickly and going outside to start and warm the truck. There were two guys, dressed in full fishing gear, leaning on the back of a Ford Explorer under the hotel portico. I waved hello and they waved back. They were our guides: Paul Jacob and Norm Raffelson. Each looked the part. Both were in decent shape, of average height, and somewhere in the neighborhood of thirty-five to forty years old.

I went back inside to fetch Dad and my brothers. I looked down the hallway of the first floor and saw Dad closing the door to room 106. The door to the stairwell opened and there stood Chris and Mike with backpacks over their shoulders. Together we walked past the front desk and out the front door to greet our guides.

Paul was the leader of the pack of two. Even though this was our first time meeting Paul, my brothers and I felt as if we'd known Dad's favorite fishing guide for years. We've heard so much about him and have seen Dad and Paul posing together in many pictures.

"It was obvious there was a sense of urgency about this trip," Paul told me. "You could tell your dad really wanted you guys to be together. I felt really special to be a part of that."

Paul understood the father/son fishing connection and had seen it before, but not to a level where the fishing was secondary to something bigger. That doesn't mean the fishing wasn't important to us—it was. We wanted to catch as many fish as we could. It was up to Paul and Norm to put us "on fish."

We followed Paul and Norm out of the Holiday Inn Express on a drive north of Batavia, motoring through open farmland at speeds near 70. There were no cars on the road at that hour, but there were trucks heading to and from food processing plants.

Dad looked wide awake, as if he'd had a good night's sleep, which of course he did. Chris and Michael were crammed in the back of the cab with their heads down sleeping. Their eyes were shielded by the brims of their ball caps. An interesting smell was milling about the cab. It was part minty fresh, part bad breath. I had a feeling those guys might have been up to trouble.

The dark morning sky was clear with stars shining and the air crisp and cold. It was 28 degrees when we left the hotel, but the forecast was for temperatures in the low 50s before the day was done. We were dressed very warmly, and with the truck's heater cranking, we started to fight foggy windows early into the drive. It was a near constant battle with the defroster.

With the help of headlights and a near full moon, I could see leftover cornstalks tilled into the muddy clumps of otherwise flat land. Most of the homes we passed had at least one pickup parked in the driveway, and there were plenty of snow plows resting on the grass nearby. There was no snow on the ground yet, but you could tell the region could handle it when it came. This is the snow belt, after all.

Our forty-five-minute drive ended when we pulled into a nondescript gravel parking lot. Paul's Explorer kicked up just enough dust to make it look as if his tires were smoking. The crackling of the truck's tires added sound to an otherwise quiet start to the morning, and the vibration from the bumpiness nudged Chris and Michael from their slumber. I pulled up next to

Paul and let the dust settle before opening the door. When I did, I could hear the welcoming sound of running water.

Pre-dressed and also wearing waterproof neoprene waders that reached up to our chests, we still needed to add one more thing to our fishing getup. Each of us had to strap our metal "corker" spikes to the bottom of our wading boots. Putting them on isn't easy, especially when you're covered in bulky clothes and gear. So we took turns playing shoe salesman, guiding feet into place and then locking the corkers down.

With a little lunar luminance we marched down a 50-degree-grade narrow trail. We followed our ears as much as the worn path to the water's edge. The sound of our feet on the hardpan dirt had the cadence of soldiers marching in heavy boots. Crunch, crunch, crunch. Our loud, heavy feet alerted a small animal hiding in the brush. We couldn't see what was scurrying away as we approached, but we could hear the pitter patter of small feet racing across dried leaves. And we could hear the sound of the running water growing louder. It wasn't exceptionally loud, but combined with the continuous crunch of our spikes, our guides had to raise their voices to be heard.

Paul took Dad and Mike to the right side of the river while Norm took Chris and me to the left. We didn't know we would be splitting up, but the pairings made perfect sense. Chris and I reunited to fish for something bigger and better than the primitive fishing we did as children. Dad and Mike were together again, with the silence of those lonely Mom-less dinners at home replaced by the soothing sound of the river's song.

At Dad's age and with his limited mobility, Paul opted to stay near the trail head and closer to the dam at the head of the river, which I've been discouraged to identify by name. The dam's domed fluorescents threw enough light on the water that Dad and Mike could see the cold water boiling with spirals of bubbles rising from the depths and sliding across the surface. Paul told Mike to sit on a small rock near a concrete wall that lined the river for about 150 yards from the dam. He said he would be back in a couple of minutes after tending to Dad.

In the dark Mike sat, shivering in the cold, with the sound of the river threatening to lull him to sleep. He had forgotten to wear his long underwear top, and his head was fuzzy. Tired, cold, and quite possibly hung over is a tough way to start the day while sitting on a slippery rock and hoping not to slip off.

The tree-lined river made for a tricky entry. Exposed roots grew down the slopes and into the water in many places. It was a tangled, dangerous mess. One slight misstep could swallow a foot, leading to a broken ankle or worse. Paul and Dad would know about that. Dad broke his leg a few years back fishing with Paul. It was nobody's fault, but both men learned a lesson. Take it slow, take it easy, and wear corkers for better traction.

Paul stepped into the river first. Dad sat down on the bank and did a pseudo slide into Paul's arms. Once in the water, they linked arms. Paul led my dad, father and bride style, to a place where the current wasn't so strong and the river bottom wasn't so slippery. They couldn't see much in the darkness, but Paul knows this stretch of river by heart. He "sees" the underwater terrain with his feet, ears, and memory. He parked Dad about thirty yards to Mike's right downstream.

As that was unfolding, Norm took Chris and me to the other side of the river. The land was actually a peninsula surrounded by the main river where we would fish, and a smaller one behind that was mostly stagnant water. Our head lamps lit the way as we walked down a narrow path through a thick swath of trees. Had it not been late fall with all the leaves down, and other gnarly ground cover shriveled up, it would have been tough to traverse through the trees.

Here we were, as middle-aged adults, hiking through the woods of Western New York. As we did, I drifted back in time and mind to the woods of our childhood where Chris used to take me fishing for crayfish and suckers. Naturally Chris was in front of me again. Norm was in front of him leading the way.

Our warm breath hit the cold air and created fog around our faces. The light from our head lamps bounced off the condensation and back into our eyes. Something else bounced back. It was that same odor I smelled in the truck on the ride in. It was minty but malodorous. I made a mental note of it on the long ten-minute march.

Our entry place along the river was a ten-foot gap in the brush. We descended down the sloped riverbank while holding onto skinny trees for support and stepping sideways to get extra traction with our spikes. We couldn't see the water very well, but from the sound of it, it was medium speed.

It was still too early to fish, so we reclined on the riverbank in very close quarters to kill time. That stale stench from the drive and hike in was growing stronger. On Chris's smoky breath rode the unmistakable scent of breath freshener. "What's with the mouthwash? You and Mike stay up a little too late?" I asked Chris.

"Maybe," Chris answered.

"Whaddaya mean maybe? Did you drink the whole bottle of Scope?"

"What's it matter?"

"I don't know that it does, unless you want to be hung over and cold."

"Nah, I'm all right. Not sure about Mike though."

"What a minute, what time did you go to bed?"

"About 1:30."

"And how much did you drink?" I asked.

"Uh ... we finished that eighteen pack."

Norm chuckled with a knowing laugh. This was not his first fishing rodeo. He knew as well as we did that the best way to handle a hangover while fishing was to catch a lot of fish. We could only hope.

Upstream Dad waited patiently, standing in the water and enjoying the massage as the current caressed his legs. Mike hadn't slipped off that hangover rock just yet, but his ass was sore and his head was aching. My head was clear but my heart was heavy. Not that I enjoy hangovers, but I would have liked to have had a chance to have one. However, I was not invited to the party in room 208.

All around us we saw bouncy halogen lights. Parties of fishermen walked with heavy feet, crushing dried leaves and small branches as they searched for their preferred spot. I would have preferred to sleep in for another couple of hours, but based on the volume of foot traffic we saw and heard, it was wise to get up early to secure our prime spots. We hunkered down to wait, and wait some more.

Right around six the wait was over. There was just enough light to see, and the crack of dawn is always a good time to fish. Fish are like waking people, grumpy and ferociously hungry in the morning. Upstream, Paul was ready to rumble. He made his first cast of the day into the ripples of the river, with a bead masquerading as a fish egg. He was testing the current and water depth more than anything else, but just like that, a fish took a bite. Fish on! A good early sign.

"Hey, Michael. C'mon over here," Paul instructed.

Michael slid over from his perch on hangover rock and took the rod from Paul. Mike hadn't done much fly fishing in his life prior to this trip, so Paul coached him through the fight step-by-step. About ten minutes later an eight-pound brown trout was in the net and a fish was on the board. Not so fast. Mike wasn't about to take credit for such an easy catch.

"I gotta hook him myself for it to count," Mike said out loud before releasing the fish back into the river.

As much as Dad appreciated Mike's true fisherman's spirit about what counts and what doesn't, he really wanted someone in the family bunch to get the first "true" catch of the day so we could get some momentum going.

With rod in hand and Paul's voice in his ear, Mike got a strike on his own in just a couple of minutes. A good cast led to a smooth drift and a ferocious strike. The float indicator ducked underwater. In a move equal parts pushing and pulling, Mike flicked the rod 45 degrees to the right downstream. The green fly line jumped out of the water, instantly taut. The vibrating of the fly line shook water droplets off in near perfect symmetry.

Dad saw the whole thing and was *beaming*. The opposite forces of Mike lifting up and the fish pulling down made the rod dance and Dad's heart sing. Mike's heart was in it too. Maybe a little too much, and in the wrong place. With a lump in his throat and the fish lumping and jumping along, Mike must have said to himself, *Just get it in.*

"Turn your body in the direction he goes," Paul said, while splitting the distance between Mike and the fish.

It was a nervous fight for Mike and the fish, and for Paul and Dad. After a couple of minutes the fish had tired and was rolling on its side. Mike reeled in about halfway and turned the rod in the direction of Paul, who was standing on the side of the stream with the net ready. Paul grabbed the leader with his left hand and scooped with the right. Mike's first "real" fish, a gorgeous six-pound green and sleek dotted missile steelhead was in the ledger. Dad looked up from his spot and saw a look of wonder and accomplishment on his youngest son's face that said, "I did it!"

That "look" consummated the trip and lifted the burden that all fishermen face.

"I was worried about all three of you," Dad said. "That's part of being a parent. I was just happy in general, and happy it was the first fish. You are nervous until you get that first one. I was relieved. Paul was too. Mike got it in. That's all that matters."

Downstream Chris and I were ready to go too. The stretch of river where we were is about thirty yards wide. The water was cold, gun metal gray in color. There was a "nervous" section of ripples directly in front of us that stretched for about fifty feet. It just looked like a place where we'd be "on fish."

Directly across from us was a father and son. The dad was about fifty and the son thirty. To their right were two brothers in their early twenties. And on our side of the river, upstream to the right, were two septuagenarians named Jack and Bob. Everybody looked like there was no place they'd rather be.

Chris and I used the same egg patterns—plastic beads—that Dad and Michael were using about 250 yards upstream. Norm squeezed three tiny split shots onto the leader about two inches above a small hook. The split shots made the egg sink, and the orange foam strike indicator would let us know if we had a bite.

There were trees close behind us, which made backcasting impossible. On top of that there was a thick bush within arm's reach to my right. It was a tough place to fish, but a good place that was worth the challenges. Norm told Chris and me to roll cast on the backhand just above the gentle rapids, letting the line drift downstream and across stretches of bubbled "feeder lines." It sounds easy, but there was effort.

I started by pulling about twenty feet of line off the reel, letting the slack float in the water in front of me. The jumbled line did me no good between my waders. I had to generate momentum in a tight space to cast it away. This was where art, skill, and imagination would unfold. I lifted the rod tip to eleven o'clock and drew a skinny teardrop across the face of a clock. I pulled down diagonally and to my right toward four o'clock, turning my wrist to the left to increase torque. Scooping around to the left, I traced the outside edge of the clock between four and eight.

Just past eight I rotated my wrist back to the right while lifting up. The rod tip followed a steep path on the inside of the numbers back to eleven where the cast started but wouldn't finish. There was one more move to make in the direction of one o'clock. I snapped my wrist to the right, drawing a candlewick out of the top right of the teardrop, firing the fly in the direction where Norm instructed.

Now the clock ticked, rather quickly I might add. If we saw the strike indicator disappear, we were to pull low and downstream. In this case that was to the left on the forehand. The idea was the fish were swimming, or holding their places facing upstream, while gobbling eggs that floated down. A low set to the left pulled the hook into the fish's mouth. A pull to the right pulled the hook out.

After a couple of casts and mending the line to keep the slack upstream from the egg, my strike indicator disappeared. It had been doing a consistent up and down dipsy doo through the rapids, but on the tail end of a bubbled feeder line, it dipped but didn't do. I pulled the tip of the rod down and to the left. Something pulled back. Fish on, baby!

I took a deep breath and enjoyed the instant high that made every cell in my body tingle. I felt my hair trying to stand up under my hat. My hands were trembling because the fish was pulling. My heart was racing and my stomach was cartwheeling. I didn't want to rush, but the adrenaline burst was trying to force the issue.

"Nice and easy," Norm said quietly. "Reel in the slack and keep some tension on him. If he runs, let him go. The drag is set on the reel. He won't get too far."

Norm's voice was the calm I needed in my personal storm. I was happy as could be, but nervous as hell. Every fisherman knows that awful feeling of a fish getting off the line. Your hands go soft, the line goes slack, and your heart drowns. I'll say this about this fish, it had a lot of heart. The fight was initially fast and furious, but the fish switched it up. It stalled and sat on the river bottom. I wasn't sure whether to start reeling in or to try to lift him out.

"Keep the rod tip up to keep the tension on. He'll start moving again," Norm said.

Norm was right. The fish headed left toward where Chris's line was with its dorsal fin slicing through the water. Chris saw it coming and pulled his line out of the way to prevent a tangle. The trout nearly beached itself but thought better of it. It splashed Chris and reversed course at twice the speed and force. It pulled so hard it straightened the right angle of my bent arm from Cape Cod to Long Island.

To get the rod tip vertical again, I pulled my elbow in, digging it into my ribs. The simple move in gave me twice the leverage. I could feel the fish tiring and we could see more of its body as it swam parallel to the shore, instead of in and out, or up and down.

"Okay start reeling," Norm said.

The fish was heavy. Though it couldn't muster much of a fight anymore, its body bowed like a crescent moon, which made it feel twice as heavy as it really was.

"Turn the rod tip over toward me," Norm instructed as he stood in knee-deep water. He grabbed the leader of the line with his right hand and scooped with the left. The fish gave a few more flops in the net, but with nowhere to go, it was all mine.

A surge of dopamine sent euphoria through my body. It was pure joy and a great relief. I was so worried I would mess it up. It was a good-sized fish at five pounds and eighteen inches, and it fought out of its weight class.

Chris looked over and grinned. At least I think he did. It was hard to say for sure because the dip inside his lower lip was so big he could hardly close his mouth. With a mouthful of dip and saliva, he spat into the river, wiped tobacco flecks off his lip, gave a thumbs up, and quickly roll cast back into a feeding line.

Norm pulled out his digital camera and snapped off a couple of shots of the brown trout with speckles. Then I put the fish back into the water, gently reviving him before he snapped his tail and slid out of my hand. I feasted on the adrenaline.

The sense of wonder, accomplishment, and profound joy that fishing brings me reaches deep into my bones. I suppose others feel this way too, even if they don't express it quite the same way in word. You can tell by their look how much catching a fish means to them. I live to fish, not the other way around.

Even though I've known him my whole life, I'm having trouble reconciling the man to my left. He is my brother, but is he my friend? Watching my brother Chris fish is an exercise in dichotomy. The peace that fishing brings to him makes him look like a totally different person. The look of stress that he wears even when he's not feeling any is gone.

His casting is beautiful and precise, despite nerve damage in his right hand that makes shaking hands for him very painful. Nobody knows the root of the problem, which caused his fingers to curl and robbed his dominant hand of about half its function. Two surgeries to fix it didn't work out. But his bad hand is better than most other people's good hands when it comes to fishing. If you didn't know, you wouldn't know. He hides his hand problem well.

A couple of minutes after my first catch, I heard a fish tail slapping the surface of water about fifteen feet below the nervous water. I looked over at Chris and his rod was springing around. He, however, was very still. He held the rod tip up and let the equipment absorb the power of the pulling fish. The fish worked its way back upriver toward where my cast ends. He did it for me, so I did it for him—I reeled my line in to avoid a tangle.

Norm was creeping along in ankle-deep water, tempted to talk, but knowing Chris had a good idea of what to do already. The fish jumped, giving us a good look at its size. It was a nice one, but it was hard to make out its colors from this far away because there still wasn't much light. The fish made another run toward the other side of the river where two brothers about twenty years younger than Chris and me were fishing side by side. They too brought their lines in, giving Chris's fish room to roam.

After a couple more jumps and splashes, the fish was fatigued. For five minutes Chris let the fish do pretty much whatever it wanted, only taking care to hold the rod tip up to keep tension on the line. Now it was time to reel in. The crackling sound of the reel was inconsistent because, now that the fish was being pulled in a direction that it didn't want to go, it suddenly wanted to fight some more. This fish was a champ. Chris stopped the reeling and let the fish swim a circle in the center of the river where it bended to the left.

"Okay try the reel again," Norm instructed, holding the net and inching thigh deep in the water.

Chris started reeling and the fish finally had no fight left to give. Norm asked Chris to turn the rod tip toward him. My brother did as he was told, and Norm grabbed the leader. He pulled the monofilament line closer and took a careful scoop out of the river. The fish on the line was almost as long as the frame of the net is wide, so Norm had to angle the net to land the trout. It was tricky. If you don't scoop cleanly, you lift the fish, which reduces the tension on the line. This is when the fish can spit the hook and pull the sweet cup of nectar from your lips too. But Norm got it right, and ultimately Chris did too. The fish was in, and Chris was in the game.

After Norm dug the fly out of the trout's mouth, he told Chris to grab a mesh glove that was attached to the frame of the net to put on his hand. The mesh pattern gives you a better grip when handling a slippery fish. I watched as Chris reached into the net and pulled the fish out. He did it firmly, but gently. His little squeeze kept it from flopping around, preventing injury. This is when might is right. This is a huge man who understands the fragility of smaller creatures. How he fishes is how he played with me all those years ago. Nothing brutish about it.

Chris held the fish up. It was a beautiful brown trout. There was a hint of yellow in its brown hue, and black speckles ran from its gills to the base of its tail. It was about twenty inches long and six or seven pounds. When Norm was done taking a picture, Chris released the fish into the water. He looked over at me, shook the cold water droplets off his hands, and smiled. He was happy.

Upriver Dad would have been happy to get in on the action too. He'd been working his new handmade bamboo rod for about ten minutes, but so far had nothing to show for it. He's patient. How can he not be? After spending about sixty hours making his own fly rod, he can wait a little longer. He wanted to see if the rod was as functional as it was pretty.

He cast to the left on his forehand. The sound of the homemade rod slicing the air had a decidedly lower pitch than the lighter graphite rods that Paul and Norm brought for us. The bamboo rod was stiffer too. Dad's eyes followed the flow of the strike indicator as it slid downstream. The light was improving as the sun rose over the canopy of the trees. And just as the visibility changed from just enough, to quite good, a fish rose next to the feeder line that Dad floated his egg pattern down. At least he knew there was a fish nearby.

Dad lifted his line and cast a little farther out this time in the direction of ten o'clock. He did a fast calculation of where the cast needed to land so the drift would reach the spot where he saw the trout rise. Dad pointed the rod tip directly at his strike indicator and traced its movement. Eleven o'clock, twelve, one, two and ... just before the cast was over at three, WHAM! The float was pulled underwater. Dad flicked his rod to the right, confident that he pulled the hook firmly into the mouth of a hungry fish.

"There he is," Paul said, acknowledging that his longtime client had made a good set.

The fish made an immediate run and Dad let the strong fish pull line off the reel. He headed down in the direction where other fishermen lined the river.

"Oooh yeah," Dad said quietly, knowing it was a good-sized fish, but not wanting to be overly enthusiastic. "I don't like it when other people whoop and holler. That's not right. Fishing is peaceful. It's between you and the fish," he reminded us.

Okay, so Dad hasn't seen *Wicked Tuna* on National Geographic Channel. But his fish was making plenty of noise of its own, thrashing about in the open water, violently shaking its head in the effort to break free from the hook wedged in the corner of its mouth. The fish made a run in the direction of Mike who was enjoying watching Dad fight the fish. Halfway to Mike the fish stopped and dove for the bottom of the river. Dad wanted no part of giving it a chance to hunker down between the submerged rocks where it could chafe the line.

Dad started cranking on the reel. The fish turned its head in the opposite direction, making the retrieval about as easy as closing a large umbrella on a windy day. Still he muscled the fish in against the grain. Paul netted it, used forceps to pluck the hook free, and handed the steelhead over to Dad. He was thrilled by the christening of his handcrafted rod and his first catch of the day.

"How was the rod, Bob?" Paul asked.

"Well, it was fun, and I caught something with it," Dad answered as he released the fish back to the river. "But I think it might be a little stiff."

"You want to put it aside and use my rods?"

"Yeah I think that would be a good idea. They've always worked before."

That brought a laugh from both men, which was short lived because Michael was now locked in on his second fish of the day.

"Okay, rod up, Mike, rod up," Paul instructed as he took Dad's bamboo rod over to a safe spot on the riverbank and swapped it out for a different one.

Turning his attention back to the action in the river, Paul saw Mike had a good handle on the fish. As Paul walked the replacement rod over to the family patriarch, Dad reached for it with hardly a look. He didn't want to take his eyes off his son.

As Paul pushed against the current to join the fight, Dad stayed perfectly still with his arms folded across his chest. He let the restless river swirl around his legs, while his emotions swirled inside of him. He saw two men, the same age: the son he loves deeply, and the guide he admires greatly. It is here that he realized this is why he worked so hard for forty years. This is why he stood strong in his darkest moments following Mom's death, and this is why spending the kids' inheritance on fun stuff like this is such a kick.

Then it happened. Just as Paul was going to net what looked to be a beauty of a steelhead, it slipped off.

Mike kicked at the water and his shoulders slumped. Paul's head dropped. For a moment Dad's heart sank. What he saw unfolding above him was so close to being perfect. But levity and humility intervened, reminding us that perfect is an ideal—rarely reality.

Mike and Paul looked up from the water and at each other and laughed. It was the perfect perspective in a time of loss that could be applied in so many other facets of our lives. Mike gave Dad a little wave to let him know he was fine. With that, I imagine Dad said quietly to himself, *This could be a really good day.*

TEN

Before Fly Fishing, Bats and Bricks to the Head

Chris Walsh (left) with author and brother, Kevin Walsh, Levittown, Penn., 1976

Good thoughts come from good fishing. Nothing refreshes my mind and puts me back in balance quite like it. Feelings of joy, accomplishment, and fraternity prime the mind and make it ripe for reflection. To my left Chris was swinging his fly rod in a diagonal motion and cadence that were almost identical to mine. He was looking for fish number two. As his green fly line and trailing egg flashed across the water, I flashed back in time to when we swung things other than fishing rods around each other and at each other.

It was around Christmastime in 1973. Life was good then, and still is in Meadowbrook, Pennsylvania, a borough of Abington Township, located about seventeen miles northeast of Center City, Philadelphia. I was three years old. My older brother, Chris, was five. Younger brother, Michael, would come later in 1977. Chris was my keeper. I almost cry with laughter when I remember this story, but back then we were both sobbing with throbbing heads. We were budding baseball players, but not quite ready for hardballs and wooden bats. So my dad bought us a wiffle ball set. The ball was huge and the red bat was fat, perfect for children looking to make contact.

One day, without an ounce of animosity or concern for safety, I pictured Chris's head as a ball on a batting tee. To me it made all the sense in the world to take a swing at such an ample target. Channeling my inner Mike Schmidt, I swung at Chris's head and got "good wood on it."

Chris toppled over. He was stunned by what happened. So too was my Aunt Roseanne, who was sitting on the steps that connected the family room and the kitchen. Scared out of my wits by their reactions, I dropped the bat and froze. Chris picked up the bat and repeated what I just did—in reverse. So now you have two toddlers wailing in tears after wailing on each other.

Chris grabbed me in a tender hug. He rubbed my sore head and said between sobs, "I'm so sorry I had to do that. I just wanted you to know how it feels so you wouldn't do it again."

Who says such mature things at such an immature age?

We lived on the twelve-hundred block of George Road. Most of the homes around us were split level with quarter-acre lawns that were plenty big enough to play wiffle ball, baseball, football, tag, whatever. There was no shortage of kids to play with in our neighborhood.

The roads around us were named after the children of the neighborhood developer. We lived on George Road, surrounded by Jody Road, Sharon Road, and Herbert Road. When the school bus rolled into our neighborhood, it was mostly empty. By the time it picked up the kids on three different corners, it was full. Almost all of the kids who lived around us went to Abington Public Schools. Abington has a terrific school system academically, athletically, and socially.

The 1970s was a simpler and slower time. There was no expectation that kids should be constantly "busy" with scheduled activities that accounted for every waking moment. You went to school and you came home. You rode the bus. Hardly anybody's parents drove them or walked them to school. That wasn't cool. We had time on our hands and we hung out a lot.

The issue of parental supervision was a nonissue. Parents were around, but they weren't helicoptering over kids like they are today. Dads were at work. Moms, if they didn't work outside the home, did so inside the house. We didn't need anyone to keep an eye on us and entertain us. We did that ourselves. If a dispute arose, we settled it with words or fists.

Nobody thought anything of seeing young children walking down the street unattended. That's what we did as kids, we wandered around. There were no arranged "play dates" back then.

The term didn't even exist. You just showed up at your friend's house and you played. If you heard other kids playing elsewhere and it sounded like a better option, you just joined in.

We played in yards and out in the street. Most mothers didn't want us inside their houses because we were loud and destructive. It wasn't uncommon to have a friend show up on our doorstep saying, "My mom told me to 'get out of the house.' She said she didn't want to see me all day because 'the weather was so nice.' So that's why I'm here."

Can you imagine how that would go over in today's world? Back then, nobody felt neglected when their mother told them to get lost for the day. That was the way it was.

We used to play in the middle of the street. We were less worried then about cars than we were about the texture of the road material and tall curbs. The streets were a little lumpy. It was as if dump trucks dumped tons of half-inch squared stones, poured gray goo on top, and then turned on an oven during the paving. The road surface resembled melted marshmallows on top of pumpkin pie.

When you rode your bicycle on the streets, a steady vibration worked its way up from the tires through the bike frame and into your body. The curbs gave the streets a nice squared look, but they were murder on your ankles and bike tires. If you crashed into a curb—and we all did at some point—you were sent head over heels and wheels.

Eventually the township caught up with the times and repaved the roads with smooth asphalt. This was kid heaven. No longer did the lumpy road reach up and tackle you by the shoelaces. Bike tires lasted four months, instead of two. The roads were now as smooth as our driveways, which made everything easier. What's more, the asphalt added height to the road, which made the curbs shorter. That saved a lot of ankles and bicycle tire frames.

Jody Road intersected with George Road at a right angle on the corner of our property. George was pitched at about twenty degrees alongside our front lawn. Jody had half as much slope for the forty yards of our side lawn, flattening out just as you reached the far end of the property lines of the Wards and the Whites. With minimal visual obstructions, we could get some pretty good speed going on our bikes, skateboards, or roller skates, make a wide turn at Jody Road, and coast for another two hundred yards or so before the grade flattened and then moved slightly uphill right in front of the Mecklings' driveway.

When we felt especially daring, we'd ride our bikes straight down George Road, which increased in severity just past the edge of our grass. Once you reached the far left of the Gundersons' lawn, the slope steepened from twenty degrees to about fifty. By the time you were halfway down the hill, you were waving to the Crowthers on the right and the Zuckers on the left, going about thirty miles an hour. This was breakneck speed on our banana-seated Schwinns, but we loved it. A gentle turn to the left at the bottom of the hill in front of the Simons' house slowed the speed and allowed us to do much the same thing in the other direction. Imagine riding on the inside path of a very wide letter U tilted on its side. That's what we did.

And we fished. At the bottom of George Road was Pennock Woods, a couple hundred acres of mostly untouched forest. We didn't call it Pennock Woods. It was just "the woods." We'd take off our sneakers and socks and leave them on the bank of the tributaries to the larger Pennypack Creek. We'd roll up our Sears-bought Toughskins jeans, which cost $4.99 back then, and wade right in. There were schools of sucker fish flashing between the rocks, most in the three- to four-inch range.

Those suckers were hard to catch. There were fast and slippery, plus we never brought our fishing poles. It didn't seem practical for fish so small in a stream so tight. So we used our bare hands. We usually came away empty handed, but on the rare chance we actually caught one, we'd be left with a film of slippery slime on our palms, which we promptly rubbed off on our pants.

The fishing for crayfish was much better. Plus it paid. Chris showed me how to do it. Some of the older kids in the neighborhood taught him, and he just passed it down like he did everything else. The little brown freshwater lobsters blended in perfectly with the sandy creek bottom. They were rarely out in the open and usually under rocks. Chris would lift the rock with one hand and grab with the other. I copied everything he did.

We had to move decisively when we pulled the cover off the crayfish or it would crawl away fast. With eight walking legs, those crustaceans have some good moves. They are nimble and those front claws are sharp. Because crayfish are preyed upon by foxes and birds, they're almost always alert and ready to counterattack. When they got you, it was a pretty good pinch. But the price of a pinch was worth the thirty-cents Martin's Aquarium in Jenkintown paid for each one.

Crayfish made good cleaners of fish tanks, eating fish poop and algae on the bottom. On a good day in the woods, we could catch a couple of dozen crayfish in the creek and make seven or eight dollars for the effort. It was pure capitalism and such fun. We got paid to play.

The woods was always there and waiting for us. There was so much imagination, anticipation, and a constant sense of adventure to fill us with fun. That's why we spent hours on end there.

Chris and I never swung bats at each other's' heads after that holiday horror show with the wiffle ball bat, but it truly was a harbinger of ass-kickings to come. We had a full contact brotherhood filled with moments of do unto others as he just did unto you. That meant, get revenge; and we did, constantly.

Our poor late mother, Carole, didn't know any better. She grew up in the Bronx with a much younger sibling, Roseanne. They were sisters, so, in my masculine way of thinking, they were much more civil than we were as brothers. The child civil war that constantly unfolded in our house was rough on Mom's eyes and her heart.

Dad assured her that our fighting was normal behavior among active boys. He would know having two brothers of his own. As bothered as Mom was about us kids pounding on each other, she was also concerned about us doing it in front of other people. As long as the nonsense unfolded under our roof, it was our family secret; only it wasn't.

Plenty of other neighborhood children would come over to our house to play—and often bring their brothers. At some point there would be a disagreement. Naturally, a fight would break out. Mom was troubled twofold. She didn't want her own children blasting each other, and she most definitely didn't want Chris and me beating up other people's children. But alas, she gained a morsel of comfort when she asked our friends whether such fighting happened when Chris and I were guests in their houses. The answer was yes, absolutely yes. So we fought on.

When you're two years younger than your older brother, you're pretty much overmatched in everything. I couldn't then, and probably still can't, compete with my brother, Chris, in games involving math and computation such as cards or Monopoly. While I could match and sometimes exceed Chris in small ball games of skill, if the game involved strength, I couldn't do much to budge him.

When I got frustrated I behaved badly, often taking it out on Chris. Chris put up with a lot of my crap. But like a big old dog tolerating the smaller, younger pup in a wrestling match, there's only so much he'll take before lowering the boom.

Dad likes the story of my turning the family room into a WWF wrestling ring. It was the late 1970s and I was a big fan of the WWF, which later became the WWE. Vince McMahon was calling the action back then, wearing a powder blue three-piece suit with the WWF logo on the lapel. Jesse "The Body" Ventura was by his side screaming "McMAHON!" at the beginning of every sentence. As the wrestling action unfolded on UHF Channel 17 in the background, Chris and I grappled on the orange, brown, and black shag carpet.

I circled left and right just like the Unpredictable Johnny Rodz did in the squared circle with Sergeant Slaughter. Chris looked just as annoyed as Sergeant Slaughter did on the tube. My big brother was just standing there taking a fair amount of my sticks, jabs, and taunts. We all knew a tipping point would come. Finally Chris had had enough. He looked over at Dad, who was doubling as a referee. Dad nodded consent. Next thing I know, I'm in a sleeper hold tapping out.

Another part of being a good brother means sticking up for your sibling even when he has no right to be stuck up for. I saw this so many times with our neighbors next door. The Ward family had three sons. The older and middle sons matched Chris and me in age. Sometimes the Wards' youngest son would tag along. Now if that's not a menu for mayhem, I'm not really sure what is.

We'd alternate between their property and ours for spirited games of baseball, running the bases, and football. Noble Fir trees lined our properties. The trees were tight, but you could still squeeze through them—at a price. The toll for crossing through was an abrasion from the needles. Later we discovered it was wise to draft behind another person, letting him blaze the trail and take all the pain.

The pain wasn't limited to the border crossing. Our games were tense and often filled with profanity. Now keep in mind we were a little too young to be using such language, and not quite smart enough to keep the volume down while unleashing a torrent of invectives. We'd hear the creak of the Wards' patio door, followed by the scolding voice of Mrs. Ward calling out a son's name followed by, "Strike one!"

You probably get where this is going in the baseball vernacular. If Mrs. Ward got to strike three, one of the Ward children was "out." Actually he was "in," brought inside for punishment. The strikeout was followed by a cacophony of complaint from the offending child when he was sent to his room for a five-minute grounding.

Chris and I could never quite wrap our heads around why they called such a light punishment a grounding. It was too short. Maybe so, but as the Ward brothers often pointed out, the Walsh brothers' day-long groundings on the other side of the firs for similar offenses was probably a bit much.

We made much ado about everything with the Ward children. They were tightly wound and tight with each other, as were we. That would often lead to fights. I would start it and Chris would pull me off whomever I was pounding on. One day, while we were arguing balls and strikes during a baseball game, the bickering got especially out of hand as the Ward boys told Chris and me to, "Get off our property."

"Make us," I shouted back.

"Chris and Kevin, respect our private property rights," Mrs. Ward warned through the kitchen window. "You've been told to leave. Now if you don't, I will call your mother."

So we left, but the Ward boys continued to taunt us from the safety of the other side of the trees.

"You wouldn't be talking like that if we were still there," I barked. "Why don't you come over here and say that," I threatened.

They would have none of that, but they were still ginning things up with plenty of snide comments through the tree branches. I'd had enough and went in search of something to throw. I couldn't find a hardball, or a rock, so I went to the garden next to our outdoor patio and fetched a brick. My dad lined the garden with angled bricks that were easy to pull out of place. I came back with the brick in hand, shaking it threateningly.

"What are you gonna do, throw that at me?" the middle brother taunted. "You'll never get it over the trees."

With that I reared back and threw the brick just like I would if I were throwing practice pop flies with a baseball. It was a mighty, wobbly throw. It had just enough oomph to make it over the eight-foot-tall firs. It happened so fast. There was enough camouflage from the branches that my taunter didn't see it coming. The brick came knuckling down and bounced off the center of his forehead.

The sharp corner of the brick punctured the skin, leaving a hole. It was deep, and for a moment it was black. Then the hole turned red and wet. About five seconds later he reached up with his hand to stanch the leak. It did little to help. Blood poured from the wound and spurted between his fingers. The brick lay in the green grass, speckled with blood. I heard a scream, then saw legs running toward the patio door. A minute later Mrs. Ward's car was backing out of the driveway very fast.

I still hadn't moved from my brick launching position, stuck in a catatonic state. Chris looked over at me with equal parts horror and amusement and said with a guffaw, "Uh, we're going to be in big trouble for that."

"What do you mean we? I'm the one who threw it," I told him.

About an hour later an indignant and wounded John Ward appeared by the property line sporting a bandage right smack in the middle of his forehead. "I got four stitches in my head because of you! My parents will be calling your parents later!" he huffed before storming back into the safety of his home.

That night Dr. Ward called my dad. When the fathers get involved you know it's more serious. But both men were, shall we say, men of the times. They were not about to let one incident destroy a good neighborly dynamic between the families. Still, they wanted to identify the actual thrower.

"It was me," Chris lied, offering himself up.

Now that's being your brother's keeper!

Halfway up the river my younger brother, Michael, was fighting his third fish of the day. I wasn't half the brother to him that older brother Chris was for me. I'm ashamed to say it, but it's true. Michael was born right around the time that I bounced a brick off John Ward's head. If there was a day I wish I could have over, it was the day Michael was born in 1977. I still feel awful about it.

Chris and I shared a bedroom on George Road with yellow wallpaper and framed sports posters over each of our beds. After a long night at the hospital with my mom, my dad returned home to wake us up.

"Would you boys like to go to the hospital and say hello to your new baby brother?" my father asked with cheer in his voice.

"Yeah!" Chris said, springing from his slumber.

"Ahhh ... I'll just see him when he comes home," I answered sleepily while waving my hand in deference.

"That's not very nice," Dad scolded. "Get up and get yourself ready," he thundered, as if the original question wasn't even a request.

So we climbed into our brown Chevy Supreme and went to Abington Memorial Hospital, about two miles away. Through the window of the nursery I saw my swaddled sibling. I also noticed something blue with yellow swirls sticking out of Michael's exposed stomach.

"Why does he have Play-Doh in his bellybutton?" I asked out loud.

"That's not Play-Doh," Dad laughed, "that's his umbilical cord."

When Michael got older I picked on him. He is seven years younger and I was jealous. He bumped me from being the baby of the family. That might explain it, but it doesn't excuse it. One time I convinced ... er, bullied him in letting me do the Camel Clutch on him. It was a pro wrestling move perfected by The Iron Sheik. I sat on the small of his back, interlocked the fingers of both hands, and pulled on his chin, turning his body into the Nike Swoosh.

"Ahah, ahah, ahah," Mike mumbled.

Michael's mumbling sound sounded like staccato laughter to me, so I cinched the Camel Clutch in tighter, thinking Mike was enjoying the roughhousing as much as I was. As I leaned back for leverage, the curve in Mike's upper body accentuated. The Swoosh became the top of an upside down question mark. The cadence of Mike's "ahas" quickened. He started to tap the ground with his hands on the ground in front of him. First slow gentle taps, graduating to faster, heavier ones.

As the pace and weight of the tapping intensified, I sensed something might be wrong. So I let go of his chin, causing his face to crash to the floor. His glasses bounced off the bridge of his nose and wound up north of his eyebrows. The side arms were in his hair instead of over his ears.

"Are you all right Mike?" I asked him.

"No, I couldn't breathe. Why didn't you stop when I told you to?" he asked.

"But you didn't tell me to stop, Mikey," I protested.

"Well I tried to, but your hands were covering my mouth," he said exasperatedly. "What did you think those sounds were for?"

"I thought you were laughing, so I thought I'd give you a bigger squeeze to make it more fun."

My brotherly shortcomings weren't just limited to roughhousing. I used to tease him with a weird language that included made-up words.

"Shang Face, Pockycano," I'd say to him when I'd walk in a room and find him playing with toys or watching TV. What it meant? I have no idea. But I knew the impact. It annoyed and upset him. It's almost like someone teasing you in a foreign language. You may not be able to interpret the words, but the tone of the tormentor is enough to know it's insulting.

I should have known better. This, among other things, is probably why I don't have quite the connection with my brothers that they share with each other. Who, other than Jesus, wants to hang out with his tormentor? I should have been more sensitive and protective of Michael when he was younger. I had a perfect example to follow in Chris and I blew it.

This is my second chance and I don't want it to get away from me. As I'm thinking this, Mike landed and handled his third fish of the day. The one that got away earlier just when Paul went to net it? Mike was so over that. And as he washed his hands in the river after releasing the fish, I tried to mentally release from myself the brotherly guilt I've carried for so long. I wish it were as simple as washing my hands.

ELEVEN

Good Guys, Great Fly Fishing Guides

Paul Jacob (left) and Norm Raffelson, fly fishing guides, Western New York, 2012

"Bob, swing that line over here," Paul instructed. "I want to check something."

Dad did as he was told, an obedient client who respects authority. And when it comes to putting people on fish, Paul is an authority figure in Upstate and Western New York fisheries.

"The first time I met your dad was about ten years ago on the Niagara River. He's always fun to fish with. He's just really into his fishing," Paul told me in a telephone conversation Thanksgiving afternoon, a few days after the trip.

"I've never met anyone who knows more about fishing than Paul Jacob," Dad shared in the days before and after Paul guided us.

That's really saying something because my dad has sixty-five years of fishing experience, and Paul is half Dad's age. It's a mutual admiration society between the two. Dad has followed Paul around the world for more than ten years. He does it because Paul is a good soul and a great guide.

"He puts you on fish," Dad always told us glowingly.

Paul Jacob, one of the founders of Reel Action Fly Fishing, has been putting people on fish for the better part of fifteen years. At thirty-five, he's old enough to know how and spry enough still to chase a prize catch down a swift river.

He's not a big fellow, close to six feet tall, steely blue eyes with a kind demeanor that you'd expect from someone who loves nature as much as he does. Depending on the time of year or his mood, Paul rocks different versions of facial hair. He seems to be most partial to goatees and that's what he's got going with us on this trip. There is nothing else he'd rather do than what he's doing now. He knows this because he's done other things for a living. He worked in heating and air conditioning for a short time, but it wasn't his calling. The call of the wild and putting people "on fish" was.

"I fish every day. Even if I'm not holding a rod, I'm fishing. My clients may be doing the casting and catching, but I'm fishing too. I love it," he shares.

Paul grew up in Rochester, New York, with a brother and a sister. He is the oldest. He understands the pressures of setting a good example for the younger siblings like my brother Chris did for us. Paul also knows the value of fishing with family later in life when things settle down and we grow into our own.

"I take my brother and sister fishing every couple of years and I guide them. They enjoy it. We goof around," he says.

Paul's childhood included a family home with a view of Lake Ontario. As a young boy Paul noticed a lot of fathers and sons fishing together. He longed for the joy and camaraderie that fishing brought them and wondered why his father didn't take him fishing, even though they were so close to good water.

Fishing just didn't appeal to Paul's dad, Winfred, or anyone else in the family. Paul's break came on Father's Day. Someone bought Winfred Jacob a fishing pole. Winfred hardly used it, but Paul sure did. An unwanted gift for Dad turned into the gift that kept on giving for his son.

Paul's constant comings and goings with his dad's fishing pole in hand caught the attention of all his neighbors, and one man named Dennis in particular. Dennis was a paraplegic. Despite not having the use of his legs, he could drive a specially equipped car that allowed him to operate the foot pedals with his hands. Dennis could also fish in places that were wheelchair accessible.

He and Paul became fishing pals, sharing hours together at the pier on the Genesee River. "Dennis showed me how to cast and which lures to use. He was there when I caught my first big salmon and lake trout. He definitely got me hooked on fishing," Paul remembers.

Paul follows the sun and goes where the fish are. In the wintertime he heads south to the Bahamas where he guides and fishes for bonefish, barracuda, shark, and tarpon. The flats around the islands seem to last forever. The water is warm, clear, inviting, and full of fish. After he fishes in the snow and in rushing water that doesn't freeze only because it's moving so fast, the Bahamas is a good getaway from the greater Buffalo area.

In the summer Paul goes to Alaska where the days are long and the fishing is other worldly. Millions of salmon swim up the rivers to complete their lifecycle and spawn. Pods of large rainbow trout gorge themselves on the eggs that slip off the reds and into their mouths. It's almost impossible not to catch fish by the dozens.

When our dad comes back from his Alaska trips with Paul, he speaks like a man who just had some kind of religious experience. That may not be far from the truth. Alaska is a fishing Holy Grail for those with the dough to go. I want some of that. Guess I'll have to take up a collection.

As much as Paul and Dad have fished together, neither knew the other's back story and the role two different neighbors played in furthering each man's love of fishing. What happened to Paul with his neighbor Dennis in the 1990s is very similar to what happened to Dad in the 1940s. Dad would often grab his tackle box and fishing rod and head off to a nearby pond, usually with the company of his twin brother, Dick, and their best friend, Rodney Rowland. A neighbor noticed the parade to the pond.

"His name was Bob Kapp," Dad would tell the story. "He lived a couple of doors down from us in Montclair [New Jersey]. He was married and blessed with two beautiful daughters, one of whom became a very well-known fashion model. The Kapp girls had no interest in fishing, so in essence Mr. Kapp had no one to fish with. That is until he knocked on our door. 'Can I take the twins fishing sometime?' he asked Grandma Beth. And she said 'sure.'"

It turns out Mr. Kapp wasn't a good fisherman, but he loved to fish, and he drove my dad and his twin brother, Dick, to places they otherwise wouldn't have been able to walk or ride their bikes to. Without even realizing it, Mr. Kapp introduced Dad to destination fishing. No longer did you just fish where you were, or where it was convenient. You could go to other places where the fishing was better.

From the half-hour car rides with Mr. Kapp to the public waters of North Jersey in the late 1940s, to private professionally guided trips to Montana, Alaska, British Columbia, Canada, and Chile in South America fifty years later, Dad's search for fish has taken him around the world and ultimately introduced him to Paul Jacob.

"I didn't know that. He never told me," Dad's faithful guide told me during that same Thanksgiving Day conversation.

Norm Raffelson is from the Quad Cities area of northwestern Illinois, but calls Colorado home now. His stepfather taught him how to fish. Norm fell in love with the sport, spending much of his childhood along the banks of the mighty Mississippi River. He came to the Great Lakes area to help Paul and Reel Action during the steelhead run.

Norm is a little taller than Paul and wiry. He has a light complexion and weathered skin. By the eyeball he's six feet tall, maybe a buck sixty. It's hard to say for sure because in waders and with all that fly fishing gear wrapped around the torso, everyone looks bigger than they really are. He dips Grizzly long cut.

In the warmer months Norm guides trout fisherman throughout the Rockies. In the wintertime he skis. In between guiding gigs he waits tables. Like Paul, Norm makes his primary living off the land. It's just better that way.

"I don't like all that corporate stuff. It's just not me," he said as we reclined on the muddy riverbank during a break.

Norm lives in Vail. It's one beautiful place with two very different economies. The rich and famous come to Vail to ski in the winter, and maybe return for a week or two in the summer. They throw a ton of money around that must be stretched out for the rest of the year for the year 'rounders. It's not always enough, so the locals get creative. Trade replaces cash as currency.

"It's a barter town. We trade everything," Norm explains.

Norm strikes you as the kind of guy who made a decision years ago to live his life on his terms come hell or trout fishing water. He's a no BS guy and is not afraid to correct your casting errors and fishing foibles. I like that. He treats you well but doesn't kiss your ass. And he puts you on fish.

"See that feeder line on the inside of where the nervous water starts, Kevin?" he asked. "Cast just above that and let it drift down."

That was a place I could see and a spot that I could land an egg on. It wasn't always so easy. If Norm could see the spot, but couldn't quite verbalize it because so much of the water looked the same, he'd take my rod and cast to give me a visual.

"Right there," he'd say after landing the egg pattern on the *exact* ripple he intended to. I don't think he ever missed. He is a marksman.

Norm is left handed, which made everything he did a little more striking to the eye. He could zip a fly line three quarters of the way across the river without ever pulling the tip of the rod behind his head. He got so much distance out of so little preload. The power came from the outside torque of his wrist on the release, which produced a screwball-like fade. What's more, he could mend the line *in the air*, putting a reverse English on the original cast to keep the slacked line upstream from the bead. Watching Norm cast was like watching a billiards master manipulate the cue ball. He has amazing hands.

Upriver Paul had a cell phone in his hands. He called down to Norm to see how the fishing was where the river bended.

"Yeah it's pretty good," Norm told him. "We've got a couple already and the guys around us are catching fish too."

Out of the corner of his eye Paul caught Mike on the phone too. Except Mike wasn't talking about fishing.

TWELVE

Cell Phones Swim with the Fishes

It was midmorning and Mike was on the phone with the office. He was also in the middle of the river. The report he sent in the day before had been looked over, and there were questions. He did his best to answer them.

Mike wasn't the only one talking on a cell. Across from Chris and me, the dad from that father/son fishing combo was talking to his wife. From the "Yes honeys, oh we're fine, and love you toos," I couldn't imagine who else he'd be talking to.

To my left and between casts and catches Chris was working his phone too. He was emailing pictures back home to Texas for his children to see. His two sons were loving what they saw and wishing they were with us. Maybe someday Chris will take his children here or somewhere else spectacular to fish. I can't remember a time that I'd seen my older brother happier.

Up and down the river I saw a lot of men talking on their phones or punching their keypads. I remember a time when fishing was a way to get away from all of that. The first time I took a cell phone fishing, it got soaked. I was living in Central California and my dad was visiting. I took him up to the high Sierra to fish a mountain lake. I put my tackle box, with my cell phone inside of it, on top of a stump at the water's edge. Edison Electric had a pumping station there.

"Do you notice the water level rising?" Dad had asked.

"Yeah I do."

Just as I answered him I looked back to see my tackle box floating. The lures were fine, but the phone was toast. A week later, I drowned the replacement phone. It broke off the holster on my belt and splashed into a mountain stream near North Fork. Put a fork in it. And then while fishing for bass in Fresno at Woodward Lake, I dropped my third phone into the drink in as many weeks.

After the trifecta I figured fishing and cell phones didn't really go all that well together. Did I listen to myself? Of course not. But that's my choice.

My brother Michael didn't have a choice. He had to respond to the calls and text messages. Eventually a conference call had to be held. To the best of anyone's knowledge it was the first time a conference call took place in the middle of a fly fishing stream during steelhead season. Holding a fly rod in one hand, while pressing your iPhone to your ear with the other, in the middle of a fight with a fish is a fight in and of itself. But you do what you have to do.

Mike handled the situation at the office deftly and kept catching fish. How he didn't drop his phone in the river, nobody knows. His good fishing was a reward for his efforts in getting his work report done, and then being helpful and accessible when questions arose. Plus the fishing success was a relief for his early morning hangover.

THIRTEEN

90 Percent of Fish Are Caught by 10 Percent of Fishermen

Chris Walsh with steelhead; Kevin Walsh fishing in background, Western New York, 2012

Fellow fisherman Jack Kuyper, Western New York, 2012

By late morning I hit a dry spell. I had plenty of hits, but couldn't get a fish on the line. Chris got on a hot streak, that father/son combo across the river was pulling them in every couple of casts, and the older gentlemen to my right—Jack and Bob—were on fish too. The success unfolding around me gave me hope that my time would come again.

But the harder I tried, the worse it got. I was pulling hooks out of hungry mouths. It would have been better to let the fish hook themselves. Norm kept reminding me about gentler hook sets. "Just flick your wrist," he said with a little punch.

Norm was right, but I just couldn't help myself. I was hyper and it was affecting my fishing. I bummed a dip of Grizzly from Norm hoping that would settle me down and spark a rally in the river. No buzz in the water, but there was certainly one in my head. The nicotine rush brought on a rush of memories that were all connected to the people and visuals around me.

The father and son across from Chris and me was a perfect example of why we were here in New York and how special it is to fish with your dad. Dad was up the river paired with Mike, but Chris and I have both had plenty alone time over the years with the man who got us hooked on the sport.

As young boys in the 1970s, Chris and I loved doing guy things and going places with our father. He was a real outdoorsman who tried to instill in us a love of camping, wildlife, and fishing especially. Chris couldn't get enough of the angling. He and Dad would fish as often as they could. They'd be gone all day. When they returned I'd always ask, "How many did you catch?"

There were plenty of slim days and other times when they didn't catch a thing. It hardly seemed to bother them. "We had a great time," both would answer.

Really? I just could never quite grasp that. I found fishing to be dreadfully dull unless you were catching fish nonstop. What I never could have imagined as a child was how much my life and life in general would change over time. What seemed like a colossal bore years ago was by my late teens wonderfully relaxing. Fishing was how I unwound from the pressures of competitive sports, college academics, and eventually the working world.

But just because I learned to love fishing doesn't mean I was any good at it. That would come later with the help of someone who reminded me very much of Jack, the elderly man who was smoking a pipe off to my right.

Jack was working a fishing hole above my spot on the river. He was also working his pipe, sending puffs of smoke downwind. I can't stand the smell of cigarettes, but the sweet aroma of tobacco smoked from a pipe is quite pleasant. It reminded me of Fred Kaufman who lived in our childhood neighborhood on Herbert Road. Your nose always knew where Mr. Kaufman was even if you couldn't see him.

It's my guess that Jack has been fishing longer than I've been alive. His pipe may be older than I am too. Joining Jack was Bob, his longtime friend from North Central Pennsylvania. It's clear they've grown old together, bonding as men and friends over fishing. I wondered if that would be my future. Would fishing be the hook for a friendship with Chris and Michael that I somehow lost, or never quite had?

I had a lot of thoughts in my head while we fished. What if my brothers didn't want the same thing out of this trip that I did? What would Dad think of my thinking? He wanted his sons to be together, and it took his lead and resources to make it happen. So here we were, with an undercurrent swimming under the current in the river. How would I reel my brothers in? I didn't know, and that made me nervous. I guessed I'd just have to cast my hopes for a better future before them, much like I cast a plastic egg into the nervous water in front of me. I only wanted a nibble.

"Whoa!" I heard off to my right as Jack set a hook in the mouth of an aggressive steelhead. The water was shallow where Jack hooked on, and there was little room for the fish to run. It made as many moves as a rodeo bull inside a pen with its testicles tied up. It was fighting mad and that made for a great fight.

"Swing him over, Jack," Bob encouraged while holding the net for his lifelong friend.

Twice Bob scooped and twice the fish dodged the net. "Wow, he doesn't want to come in!" Bob laughed.

That fish had good wiggles, but it couldn't quite wiggle itself off the hook. Jack puffed away on his pipe as the steelhead huffed and puffed through the water. The sync of the smoking matched the fish's splashing. Puff, splash, puff, splash. On Jack's third try to land it, Bob slid the knotted nylon net under the fish's slippery side. He lifted up to display his pal's good fortune.

"Oh, that's a good one," Jack said just loud enough to be heard over the sound of the rushing river.

Jack and Bob have caught hundreds of fish together, but clearly the thrill of it has never gotten old. They're as seasoned as you can get, but as giddy as neophytes. As the men worked to remove the fly from the mouth of the twenty-two-inch speckled fatty, Chris came up the river to take in the spectacle. He shook his head side to side, but in a way meant to be positive.

"Those guys are awesome," Chris said with measured tone. "Look at 'em. Still friends and still fishing after all these years."

He was right. And I thought, that could be us, if we wanted it to be. Jack the Fisherman reminded me of Jim the Forester. Old Jim made me a better fisherman overnight. He was a kind soul and soul fisherman. I met Jim in the late '90s in California when I was working as a TV news anchor for the local CBS affiliate. Not only do Jack and Jim look alike, they're about the same age.

Jim was a retired California state forester. If there was a body of water in the central Sierra Nevada or the San Joaquin Valley that Jim hadn't fished, I'd be shocked.

Whenever I'd go fishing in the mountains, or anywhere else, I'd always stop by Herb Bauer Sporting Goods in Fresno to get supplies and talk to Jim first. Sometimes I didn't know exactly where I was going, or where I'd been, but if I could describe it roughly, Jim could pinpoint it exactly. He was always spot on with what lures and flies to use and how to use them.

Working on TV in the evening gave me a lot of time to fish in the morning. I did most of my fishing at Woodward Lake, a manmade lake across the street from my house on the north side of Fresno. On the weekends I'd bring Jean along. Sometimes she'd wet a worm, but she usually found the ride in the aluminum rowboat and looking at the big homes on the lake more interesting.

The fishing was usually very good as the homeowners' association had a catch and release policy, and the lake was stocked with Florida strain largemouth bass. But in the spring of 1999, I was going through a rough stretch. I hadn't caught much fish at all and was telling Jim that my luck had run cold. He wasn't buying. I'll never forget what he said. It was a two-minute conversation that had a profound impact on me.

"There's an old expression: 90 percent of fish are caught by 10 percent of the fisherman. What does that tell you?" Jim asked. "It means fishing is more about skill than it is about luck. The knowledgeable fisherman knows where the fish are and how to catch them."

I crinkled my face and tried to process that on the wrinkles of my brain. Jim took the cue and simplified.

"Look, you know those people who throw a worm and a bobber in the middle of the lake and wait for a fish to swim by and take a bite?"

"Yes. I do that sometimes."

"How does that work out?" he wanted to know.

"Not very well," I admitted.

"The reason why is fish *don't* swim around looking for food. They are where food already *is*. You need to know that or you won't ever catch many fish. You should fish where streams flow into ponds. Streams bring bugs and little bait fish into ponds and lakes, and the bigger fish are waiting there to eat them. Cast your worm, lure, or fly around structure. Fish like to hide under docks, logs, weeds. By knowing this you can eliminate about 99 percent of the water. You need to fish where the fish *are*."

I felt like an idiot, but self-knowledge is the beginning of self-discovery. So I kept listening.

"If you don't get a bite after a couple of casts, move on to another place. Change colors, lures, and flies until you find something that works. And present well, as naturally as possible. How do you use a plastic worm?" Jim asked.

"I just cast it and reel it in slowly," I answered.

While shaking his head and chuckling, Jim said, "Worms don't swim, they *drown*. Imagine you're a bass sitting on the bottom. You see a splash that gets your attention. But then you see a worm swimming away. That doesn't look right to the bass now does it? If you throw a real worm into the water, it's going to sink. While it's sinking it lifts its head. It's trying to keep its head above water. So what you want to do is cast your plastic worm; let it fall, and as it's falling gently lift your rod tip every couple of seconds to twitch the worm's head. That will look a lot more natural to the fish as he decides whether he wants to take a bite."

After a pep talk from Jim, my production improved instantly, and my fishing style changed dramatically. I went from a hopèr to a hunter. I no longer waited for fish to come to me. I stalked them, often trying to see if I could sneak up on them and actually see them in the water before I cast. This totally changed my attitude toward fishing and boosted my confidence.

Dad saw the difference the next time he and Mary came out to visit Jean and me in the years before we had children. "You really seem to know what you're doing," he remarked when I took him trolling around Woodward Lake, pulling bass in by the boatload.

"How did this happen?" Dad asked.

That's when Dad met Jim. I took him over to the store, and the two anglers acted as if they'd known each other their whole lives, even though they'd just met. Fishing does this for people. It makes friends out of strangers and builds bonds within families. That's what we've come to know, and we were hoping for more of it on our trip to Western New York.

Jim may have taught me how to catch bass, but Dad taught me how to fly fish for trout. That started back in 2003 when I moved from the West Coast back East. "Don't *ever* tell anyone the name of the river where we fish the hex hatch," Dad told me when he knew I was writing this book. There he went again. Same message, different river. "You'll mess it up, and you'll be shunned by the regulars."

By regulars he meant Gordon and all his Italian fishing friends in New England who would probably give me the *malocchio*—Italian slang for the hairy eyeball. That might be the least of my worries. Dad just might disown me. So in the interest of family unity, I won't name the place or its location. I will say this: it's equidistant between his home in Connecticut and mine in Massachusetts.

Deep in the pine barrens of the mystery state is a river that runs through it. There's no good signage around to point the way to our secret fishing spot. You just need to know where you're going, or you're going to get very lost, very fast. Dad knows the way by heart. His "fishing car," a Subaru Forrester, has taken him down the dirt roads of the New England wilderness thousands of times. No wonder the station wagon has more than 90,000 miles on it and the lub lub sound of tires that needed to be rotated about 20,000 miles ago.

Most people slow down when they off-road. If anything, Dad speeds up. So eager to fish, he leaves behind a cloud of dust that has covered many a following car or truck. He's just so excited about what awaits, even though he's done the same thing in the same place for years. It's like visiting your favorite ice cream parlor and ordering the same flavor over and over again. It never gets old, even though you do.

This flowing water is more a stream than it is a river, not much more than fifty feet wide. The current is gentle and the depth ranges from knee to mid-chest high. It's easy to wade and easy on the eyes. Trees grow over it, reducing glare, but letting in just enough sun to make the reddish brown tint of the water pop. There are a couple of sandbars and fallen trees in the river, but for the most part you can wade it with little worry about underwater snags.

When I fish with Dad in our getaway spot, it's always during the hex hatch. It's beyond exciting—stimulation overload with a chance to catch a lot of fish in a small window of time. From late June through August, hexagenia flies hatch from the mud of the river bottom. The timing is as reliable as the setting sun and the evening song of the whip-poor-will bird. Whistle *whip-poor-will* three times and you have it. The birds call when the sun sets, and within minutes there's fuzz and buzz in the air.

The fuzz is hex flies. They look like miniature flying dragons with inch-long yellow bodies shaped like Js, and white puffs around their heads. They break off the river bottom, float to the top, and if they're not intercepted by a hungry fish they'll fly away. The buzz is the excitement the fisherman feels in his heart, his hands, his soul, and in every cell of his body. It's the anticipation that at any moment a brown or a rainbow trout will rise up with the rising fly and bite the meticulously tied artificial one that the angler is twitching on the water's surface instead.

I still remember the first time I fished the hex hatch with Dad. It was a warm night in late June 2003. The air temperature was about 85 degrees. The water temperature much cooler. I was excited to get into the water to fish and to cool off.

The fishing turned out to be hot. Ahead I heard a splash, followed by the pitter patter of a fish's tail. I saw my dad turning in the direction of the fish's getaway. He was holding the rod in his right hand, the fly line in his left, and the tip of the rod was bending like a curlicue. The fish turned left and headed up river toward me. He wouldn't make it halfway because of the tension on the line. Dad knew he had the first fish of the night and he looked happier than a pig in slop.

The fish slapped around some more before Dad reeled him in for good. He reached down with his left hand and gave the creature a gentle squeeze that secured it in his fingers and diagonally across the crook of his wrist. Fish in hand and reel now tucked under his right arm and side, Dad used his right hand to undo the small hook from the rainbow's lower lip. Dad felt not only the thrill of his catch, but also the joy of witnessing the sincerest form of flattery. Fifty yards away, I had hooked my first fish of the night.

As the whip-poor-wills whipped themselves into a mating and singing frenzy, the fish and flies did too. Clouds of hex flies hovered above the water and the fish raced to fill up on them. There were splashes everywhere as the action became orgasmic. We'd see a splash, cast toward it, and catch a fish. Dad pulled them in in bunches. I did too.

The clocked ticked on available light, and what we could no longer see with our eyes, we caught with our ears. Bloop, bloop, bloop went the sounds of striking fish on rising flies. Sometimes it happened right between our legs. That would give anyone a rise. And on that first night when the sky was almost black, just fifteen minutes after the hatch had started, I caught a brown in close. I didn't even have to reel. I just reached down and plucked him out of the water.

The sound of the whip-poor-will song was silenced and replaced by the sloshing sound of Dad wading toward me. He turned on his head lamp and looked at my hands. The bright incandescent light illuminated the light speckles on the greenish brown top and the rich red that lined the fish's bottom.

I looked up at him and he had this pleased grin on his face. I'm pretty sure I had the same look on my face too. I looked down at the fish and it looked afraid. That wouldn't last for long. I put the fish back in the water and moved it back and forth to get water and oxygen flowing across its gills. I opened my hand and the fish slowly swam away, no doubt needing a rest.

In need of a rest of our own, Dad and I headed back up the river, a twenty-minute walk in the water back to the car. When we got out of the river, waiting for us were sandwiches packed inside a cooler. It was a late-night dinner sitting on the back of Dad's Subaru with the back hatch open, rehashing the hex hatch. It was here that we started some of our best talks and future father/son bonding moments. And whether it was the first time, or the tenth time, these times were certainly better than our fishing trips on the Thames in the months after Mom died.

We've bonded as a family over fishing, but not nearly as often as all the times I fished the hex hatch with Dad in our favorite place. The last time all the brothers and Dad were together was the summer of 2007. We chartered a boat out of Groton, Connecticut, to fish for bluefish and striped bass in the Eastern Long Island Sound. Armed with a cooler of beer and a sense of adventure, we went in search of birds at the direction of our guide, Captain Jack Balint of the Fish Connection.

It was a beautiful July afternoon with little wind, calm seas, and an air temperature of about 80 degrees. We found a flock of seagulls about a mile off the coast of Little Gull Island. The birds were dive bombing on the bait fish that blues and stripers had chased to the top and surrounded. The captain drove the boat in a circle as we cast our rubber tubes into the churning water. Chris, Michael, Dad, and I caught so many fish in the eight- to twelve-pound range that we stopped counting after twenty-five. My best guess is we caught somewhere around forty fish in about two hours. Sensing we had had our fill the captain asked, "Want to do some trolling for something bigger?"

"Yeah," we answered.

"All right, lines in. Let's take a ride down to Fishers Island," he said.

Fishers Island, New York, is home to the richest of the rich with mansions and guest houses perched on cliffs overlooking the Atlantic. Although just two miles off the coast of Connecticut, it is a hamlet of New York dating back to royal charters in the 1600s. It is where the Rockefellers, Roosevelts, Firestones, and DuPonts "summer"—making a verb out of a season.

On the twenty-minute ride south, I downed a couple of Sierra Nevada Pale Ales to celebrate my good fishing fortune. By the time we reached the trolling area, which was only about a hundred yards off the shore of a very private beach, I had to add to the ocean level. With respect to the women and children playing in the surf and on the sand, I waited until we drifted behind some exposed rocks.

What I didn't see until after the relief effort had started was a fifty-something-year-old man fishing on the other side of the rocks. He looked as if he had walked right out of an Eddie Bauer catalog, as if you have to look good to fish. He also looked pissed off that someone was pissing in the waters of his backyard. I waved hello. He gave a get-out-of-here wave back. It may have been his land, but this was the world's water. He couldn't have felt any better when I landed a thirty-eight-pound striper that would have been his, if it wasn't mine first.

Stoked and sunburned we called it a day soon after that. The captain floored his Evinrude 300-horsepower motor and headed back for the harbor. As the motor sucked in the petroleum, my brothers and I sucked down a few more cold ones. Dad kicked back in the back of the boat pleased as punch. He was happy to see us happy and probably wondering how long it would be until he and his sons were all together fishing again. Now we know, five years.

It felt like five years since I last had a fish on in the river here with Chris and Norm, but just before lunch time a fish decided to impale itself on my hook. It hurtled through the drink, with a couple of jumps and splashes.

"There you go, now you're back," Jack said encouragingly, through clenched teeth with pipe smoke pouring out of the corners of his mouth.

I got the fish in and felt worlds better about myself. Chris smiled and Norm did too. Upriver Jack pulled out a camera and clicked away.

FOURTEEN

Brothers Inside and Outside the River

Author Kevin Walsh with 38-pound striped bass. "Biggest fish I've ever caught. Catching it next to annoyed industry tycoon's personal fishing spot? Even better!" Fishers Island, New York, 2007

◂ Kevin (left) and Chris Walsh with fish on at same time, Western New York, November 2012

▸The Reilly Brothers (left to right) Hugh, Michael, and Will, golfing pals and lifelong friends, Huntingdon Valley, Penn., 1985

After the catch it was time for lunch and beer. Norm left us at the river and brought back the best gas station meatball sandwiches known to man. He also had a six-pack of Labatt Blue tall boys, the same brand that Chris and Mike had more than their fair share of the night before.

"Kevin might have preferred some foofy microbrew in a bottle," Chris teased. "He's one of those *craft* brew guys."

Norm looked at me with the expression of a man who had just bitten into a lemon. "Well, there's your beer right over there," he said while shaking his head and pointing to the beer on the ground.

It was funny and it was Norm. Like I said, he's a no BS guy.

"You know, you're the first people who've ever requested beer at lunch," Norm said with a laugh before taking a huge bite into his sandwich.

So we had two firsts to our family name—Mike's conference call while standing in the river and my call to send Norm on a beer run. The beer hit the spot and washed down the meatballs. As we took a break from our fishing, we watched the two brothers fishing diagonally across the river from us. They were in their early twenties, about the age that Chris and I were when we became closer again after drifting apart during our teen years. What happened within our family ranks? I guess more than anything there was a healthy dose of sibling rivalry that at times wasn't so healthy after all.

When Chris and I reached high school, we realized being friends with each other wasn't really an option. It was about as cool as brown bagging a homemade peanut butter and jelly sandwich in the school cafeteria. At some point you want more flavor out of food, life, and friendship than what your brother and PB&J brings. Our expanding appetites meant less time for each other. Plus, being just two years apart put us in the inevitable position of supremacy challenges.

Sophomore year was the first time he and I were together in the same school in six years. Abington Senior High School comprised the tenth, eleventh, and twelfth grades. I was extroverted and a good athlete, which gave me appreciable social currency. Chris was more subdued. Even though we played on the same lacrosse team when I was just a sophomore, he didn't want me hanging out with the upper classmen off the field. It would have cut into his chi.

I understood that and minimized the snubbing. But I snubbed back harder in our lives away from high school. Let's be honest about something—just about everybody I know lived a double life in the high school years. Who we were at school wasn't the same person we were at home.

It's not that Chris ignored me in the hallways of our high school; in fact, I'm pretty sure he took extra effort to keep an eye out for me on the sly. At home he was quite conversational with me. He shared stories about his life and his friends, what they did and where they went. I did a lot of listening. He left the door open for me to reciprocate, but I never did. I treated my personal life like I did my toys. I didn't want to share.

Here's the rub: when someone reaches out to you, and you don't reach back, you've left them hanging. That's exactly what I did with Chris.

And Mike? He was so much younger. He just sort of did his own thing. I didn't pay much attention to him. When I did, I was usually making fun of him or flicking his head and earlobes with cocked fingers. I'm not proud of that.

The thing I like about aging is this: it throws appropriate context right in your face. Family is everything, little things mean a lot, and little people aren't so little anymore. My God, I only have to look over at my little brother, Michael, to see him towering over me now. And you know what else? I rediscovered my brothers as good, fun people; just like I've rediscovered peanut butter and jelly as a mighty fine sandwich.

I liked what I saw with our brotherly counterparts across the river. They were catching fish and basically doing what brothers with healthy relationships do: enjoying company while trying to get a rise out of each other. To see that happening as fish rose and took flies was as golden as the mid-afternoon sun reflecting off the sparkling river.

One brother looked to be a couple of years older than the other, and my best guess is they were Native American. With Seneca and Cayuga tribe roots nearby, it was entirely possible. The older brother was a bit taller and wore a bright green ball cap. He stood on a rock and cast streamers, opting for a strip instead of a drift. There was more casting room on the opposite side of the river, and based on the eyeball, these young men could really sling it.

They were smart and they knew the river. They changed flies often to keep it fresh for suspicious fish. As a result they caught a ton of steelhead and browns.

The younger brother was doing most of the netting, because the older brother was doing most of the catching. Hmm ... sounds like what was happening with Chris and me. Chris it seemed caught two fish for my one. The difference was, Chris wasn't reminding me of the catch differential like the big brother across the river was doing to his little bro. Maybe that's the maturity that comes with age. If we took twenty years off our lives, Chris would have been busting my balls too.

Seeing brothers spending time together made me think of my own. How were we the same, how were we different, and how did we compare to the other brother combinations around us? Let's face it, we all do the comparison.

We had some very special friends growing up. They were the Reilly family from Huntingdon Valley, Pennsylvania. The Reillys have a family business. They manage and operate golf courses. The older brothers, Will and Hugh, are serious golfers just like me. Will is older than Hugh by a year, and the oldest son in a family of three boys and four girls. Hugh has lots of freckles, feisty bright red hair, and a personality to match. Back then the brothers were competitive and combative with each other on and off the golf course. By and large though, they were and still are exceptionally nice people.

I spent years traveling to local golf tournaments with the Reilly boys. They were fun to be with. They were my mentors and they were also my ride. The Reillys' red '78 Chevy Camaro was legendary for the places it took us and the fun we had in it. It was quite a sight when we rolled into the parking lots of area country clubs with Pink Floyd blaring and golf balls and tees tumbling out when we opened the doors. We looked decidedly non-clubby, and that sometimes prompted snickering among snobs.

But nobody in the stodgy golfing establishment laughed when they saw us play. We beat their asses. We didn't take ourselves too seriously, but we never messed around when it came to competitive golf.

No fast food restaurant drive-thru was too far for the red Camaro, and quite often there was a leftover wrapper on the floor from a previous visit. It was in the Camaro that I learned to curse like a champ, argue like a pro, and fart like a slob. I may have been five or six years younger than Will and Hugh, but they treated me as a peer and I loved them for it.

In addition to the constant sense of adventure, I really enjoyed the honesty of their raw and sometimes difficult relationship. Will and Hugh could switch from the peace of monks to the warring spirit of the Hatfields and McCoys at the drop of a golf visor or, in this case, a missed putt.

It was 1982. I was twelve. Hugh was seventeen and Will eighteen. We were playing a spirited match at The Abington Club in Jenkintown, Pennsylvania. Pat Reilly, Will and Hugh's uncle, was with us. Uncle Pat was in his late twenties, the size of an NFL lineman, and a solid golfer. The seventh hole was a short par four, just under 300 yards. Will is a big fella and a long hitter. He hit a massive drive that day that rolled onto the green and stopped two feet under the hole. It was as close to a kick-in eagle as you could get.

Hugh is half the size of Will and is relatively short off the tee. He makes up for it with scrambling and tenacity. You couldn't find a more different contrast in players, let alone brothers. Hugh hit his approach shot to about ten feet and drained the birdie putt. That made Will's eagle putt a little more interesting. Will took his time and looked at the cinch of a putt from all angles.

"Kev, c'mon over and take a look at this," he asked.

"Will, it's a straight putt. Just knock it in the back of the hole," I told him, trying to keep an easy putt easy.

Sometimes those simple putts are the hardest. Will pulled his Wilson 8802 blade putter back and swung it through the Titleist balata. The ball bounced as soon as he hit it, sending it offline. It missed low and to the left, the worst possible miss you could have.

Will stared at his golf ball, holding his follow through, stunned by what just happened. I looked at Pat. He couldn't believe it either. I looked at Hugh. He was holding back laughter. And then I looked back at Pat, and we both knew it was about to get really ugly.

"Pfftt ... pffft ... huh, huh huh," Hugh laughed, prompting Will to look over with fury in his eyes and his putter still in his hands. Will didn't see his little brother, he saw Judas. Hugh took off running and had about a thirty-yard head start. Will followed with his arm cocked. Hugh headed for the fifth tee, then toward the creek that ran through the middle of the nine hole golf course.

Hugh was always the faster of the two brothers and Will, thankfully, couldn't catch up with him. But Will had a hell of an arm. As Hugh ran back up the hill and over by the fourth green, Will launched his putter tomahawk-style. With a thirty-six-inch hit radius, it came really close. Had Hugh not ducked, it would have been messy.

Still on the seventh green, Pat looked over at me with an amused look on his face and asked, "You fight with your brothers?"

"All the time," I answered.

"Like that?"

"Well, maybe not quite like that."

"What about you?" I asked him.

"Nah, me and my brothers, we get along great."

Pat wasn't kidding. I've seen him with his brothers, and yes they get along famously. But even brothers who infamously wage war on one another often come around. And before our round of golf was done, so too were the hard feelings between Will and Hugh. They were friends once again.

The Reilly brothers were and still are good company, great theater, and an example of context for what it means to grow up with brothers in limited space. Stuff happens. You brawl and get it out of your system. To see them and other brothers fight just made the fighting I did with my brothers seem all the more normal.

"Hey, Chris, does your arm hurt?" I asked as he took a break from the casting.

"It's throbbing," he answered. "What about you?"

"Same thing," I told him.

Because of the side of the river we were on, and the direction of the current, we had to cast exclusively on the backhand and mend the line constantly with a series of mini lifts and loops. With each cast lasting about twenty seconds, and factoring in three mends per cast on average, we did a windshield wiper motion to the right 1,710 times that day! No wonder our shoulders hurt. My pride hurt more though because I didn't have another fish on until late in the afternoon. And then just as we went to net the near landing, the fish slipped away. I really needed some beer after that.

Mike could have used a beer too. The cell phone volley with the office took a lot out of him, but the fishing success was worth celebrating. As much fun as the fishing brought him when he could focus on that alone, Mike enjoyed watching Dad fish. Seeing his old man in his glory and catching fish easily was such a contrast to the difficult and lonely times they spent together when it was just the two of them following Mom's death in Michael's freshman year of high school.

Here father and son were together again, just the two of them. It was just like it was years ago, but this time they were together by choice, and joy had replaced despair.

Together, Chris and I caught nine fish. He landed six, I had three—four if you count the one that slipped the net. Dad says if you touch the leader of the line, it counts. I don't know about that. I know this, it was a good day either way. After reeling our lines in, Norm led us out of the brush and up the hill where Mike, Dad, and Paul were already waiting.

Dad was sitting on the tailgate of the truck. Mike was helping him take his boots and waders off. Off to the side Paul was checking over the fly rods and preparing them for the next day. As the sun set on this day, we were all ready to settle in for the night. It was a good day that delivered fish and time well spent among family. Dad looked dog tired. So did the rest of us. We would all need something good to eat and a good night's rest to be ready for more fishing the next day.

Mike drove back to the hotel. We didn't talk much on the ride because we didn't have to. We were tired and content. Our original family mission of reconnecting and retracing our family roots was accomplished. However, my personal goals of achieving brotherly friendship and forgiveness were still very much unresolved. Dad had no clue. He quickly dosed off, probably dreaming about the fishing and more time with his sons tomorrow.

Mike looked back in the rearview mirror. He grinned at me and nodded happily. I looked over at Chris and he gave me a double-raised eyebrow. I liked what I saw and loved that my brothers put some passion into the nonverbals. And as the truck quietly lumbered through the cold, sparse farmland, I thought the seeds for a warmer future might very well have been planted then and there.

FIFTEEN

Fish Out of Water, My Dad at a Bar

Jean and Kevin Walsh, Wilmington, Del., 2007

After we got back to the Holiday Inn Suites, we all retired to our rooms for showers and a change of clothes. We went to Alex's Place for dinner. The guy behind the front desk said it was famous for ribs. That was all Dad needed to hear. Alex's was a warm and woody place that reminded me of a ski lodge with better food. Located across the street from Batavia Downs, it attracted a mix of track winners and town folk who came to Alex's for comfort food.

There was a wait to be seated, so we went to the bar. I was hoping there would be a local brew for my consumption and to annoy my brothers with a spirited discussion of why craft brews are better spirits. No such luck. There was, however, Yuengling on tap. Anyone with Pennsylvania beer drinking roots ought to know Yuengling Traditional Lager comes from the oldest brewery in America. I ordered a pint and toasted my dad and my brothers.

Off to our left and under a flat screen TV was a group of women drinking white wine from gigantic glasses. It was a bachelorette party. The women were refined and well dressed. There was no tiara on the head, or sash around the shoulder and waist of the bride-to-be. Even though there were a lot of tasseled shades hanging from light fixtures, which look exactly like the fish stocking stripper leg lamps that are fixtures in bachelor pads, this place is otherwise classy.

The bar at Alex's Place is far classier, in fact, than the last bar I was in with my brothers, which, by the way, was for Mike's bachelor party in 2006. That was a great time and a beautiful wedding. I was proud to be a part of the small wedding party, which included Chris and me and the sister of Mike's wife. I didn't go to Chris's wedding and that's another brotherly do-over I'd like to have.

In 1994, I started two important phases in my life, marriage and working in television. After dating Jean Gnap for almost four years and with her father's permission, I asked her, a fellow Purdue alum, to marry me. She accepted and we married that September, not long after I took a television reporter's job with a cable TV station in the U.S. Territory of Guam. I was finally doing the work that I always wanted to, and the prettiest girl I knew was along for the ride. We just had to go to the other side of the earth to get the experience that I would need to build a career.

Guam was a wonderful place to be young and spirited. It's a tropical island in the western Pacific with a year-round average temperature of 81 degrees. The land is beautiful, and the island is surrounded by a barrier reef. The water is very warm, exceptionally clear, and filled with colorful fish. The ocean water is among the saltiest in the world, making it very dense. That makes swimmers super buoyant. You can practically sit up in the water at Tumon Beach, as if you're lounging in an invisible chair.

Jean and I loved living on the island. Sure it was impossibly far away from our families and friends whom we missed terribly, but I think the isolation of the place strengthened the bonds that helped us in the early stages of our marriage. Without the pressure of family commitments such as birthday parties and holidays, we spent so much time together, just Jean and me. We cherished that.

We were young and adventurous. We didn't have much money, so we did a lot of stuff on the cheap. We took hikes in the mountains and jungles together, careful not to tangle with brown tree snakes. We went to the beach almost every weekend. The nightlife in Tumon Bay was terrific. We danced like we did when we were back in college.

Guam's news was challenging and very international. Though we were living on American soil, many of the events in Asia shaped our news coverage. I reported by day and anchored by night. We shared our local coverage with CNN International. That meant our families and friends back on the mainland could see me on TV from time to time. They got such a kick out of that, and it was proof that I really was on TV and not goofing off on the other side of the globe.

My older brother, Chris, got married while we lived in Guam. Unfortunately I couldn't attend the wedding in New Jersey. I felt awful. The reality was I just couldn't swing it financially and logistically. You need at least a week off for a trip of that length, and the airfare was astronomical. Plus I had used up all of my vacation time for my own wedding in Chicago.

Chris married Suzanne Finaldi, a lovely Jersey Shore gal who, like Chris, once worked for Merrill Lynch. They settled in Jacksonville, Florida, before later moving the family to suburban San Antonio, Texas. There's no grudge held by them, or anyone else in the family for my not going to their wedding. When you're as far away as we were, people view you in a military overseas hardship context. It's all but assumed you'll miss out on friends and family blessings. I wish it could have been different.

As I indulged and chatted with my brothers in the bar, I realized it had been a while since we'd taken a picture together with Dad. Now was as good a time as ever, so I asked a woman who was waiting for a table with her family if she'd do it for us. I put my iPhone on camera mode and gave her a quick tutorial on how to use it. I stood behind Chris, Mike, and Dad, which made me look even shorter than I already am. We struck poses. Wait a minute, there was a pause in the action. The mom was having trouble with the technology. She couldn't do it.

"I got it," her teenaged son said, coming to the rescue.

Dad just laughed at what unfolded with the photography as he caressed his iced tea. He was having the time of his life. Talk about a fish out of water, Dad hardly drinks. I've never seen him in a bar before.

"Walsh family, party of four?"

"Yes, that's us," Dad answered.

We followed the hostess to our table near the middle of a wooded walled dining room. We were up against a wall and close to a raging fireplace. Mike sat next to Dad as he often does without even realizing it. Chris sat next to me. It was a relaxing dinner with a focus on food and family.

Dad went for ribs. Chris and Mike had beef on weck sandwiches—which are a way of life in Western New York. I had steak. The food, company, and ambiance were fabulous. When dinner was mostly done, our waitress asked if we'd like coffee and to see the dessert menu. I said, "Yes."

I was already quite full, but I never skip dessert on vacation. Chris and I split a brownie and vanilla ice cream.

As we picked through the dessert, I noticed Mike still wasn't done with his meal. He's always been slow when he eats, and even his wife, Rachel, will tell you that. I don't know why, but I watched Mike closely for a minute. He spent a ton of time pushing his food around his plate. A simple cut, stab, eat scenario doesn't exist in his world. It's almost like the beef scraps have to do a couple of laps before it's time to chew. And then when it's time for that, he's not exactly fast either.

By the time Chris and I were done with dessert and coffee, Mike was just about finished with his entree. There would be no dessert for him. The bill was already paid and Dad was itching to go. Mike's way of eating is peculiar and familiar. Somebody else we knew used to eat just like that.

SIXTEEN

Meet My Mom, Carole

Left to right: Joanne Valentine, Lesher Valentine, Chris Walsh, Carole Walsh, Dinny Van Buren, Judy Gordon and Walt Van Buren, Huntingdon Valley, PA, 1990

I've made references to her already, and now it's time for you to meet our mom. There was just something about the way Michael ate his dinner that triggered the memory of our mother doing the same thing. Except she did it with cheese omelets. I thought about her the whole ride back to the hotel.

Mom could make a day out of a meal. When we'd go out for Sunday brunch after Mass, it took forever. Mom would cut off a tiny piece, push it around her plate, look around the restaurant, wave hello to a small child, engage in conversation with Dad or the server, push the same piece around the plate a little longer, and eventually eat it some five minutes later. Young, hyper boys hardly have the patience to sit through hour-and-a-half meals.

When we got older, we started taking two cars to Mass and brunch. That way my brothers and I could leave the country club or the Warminster West Diner when we were finished eating. Mom and Dad didn't mind because they had some alone time after the family time.

"I am not your friend, I'm your *parent.*"

Mom always did have a way with words. Her love was tender at times, tough in others. "You don't have to like me, but you will *respect* me."

We did. Mom was a gritty city kid. She was born in 1940 and raised in Parkchester in the Bronx. As far as we know she never tried fishing. She never really got our need to fish, but she tolerated it. Fishing for Mom was buying scallops from fishmongers.

We always thought about where she grew up near Saint Helena's Church with a sense of mythical wonder. We pictured in our minds images of a black-and-white film documentary, one in which the children wore the same dour expressions as the adults. Life was tough. There was no need to pretend it wasn't.

Dad was Mom's ticket out of the city. After growing up inside a small apartment, she always wanted a house in the suburbs. Dad gave her that, but you know the old saying, "You can take the girl out of the city, but you can't take the city out of the girl?" That was Mom. As tough as she was, she was incredibly loving and sometimes smothering. She was constantly lassoing me and my brothers. She'd hug us, kiss us, and pinch our cheeks until they were red. This could happen anywhere: at school, church, the grocery store.

"Mom, get off! Why do you do that all the time? It's so embarrassing," I'd protest.

"I do it because I love you so much. I never want you to feel as if you're not loved enough. Some children don't have parents who love them."

She had a point and we all knew it. We loved her back. She eventually cooled it with the public displays of affection as we got older. Mom wasn't just a mother to us, she was a mother to our friends. She especially loved my best friend Steve Smolda. Boy, did he ever love her back. Steve was with me and Michael on that fateful day in the spring of 1985.

That year was an overlap of my freshman and sophomore years of high school. Ronald Reagan was in his second term as president, Pete Rose became the all-time hits leader in Major League baseball, and Madonna had two number one hits that year: *Like a Virgin* and *Crazy for You*. I was hitting the ball crazy good on the golf course, playing number one on Abington Senior High School's varsity team that almost went undefeated in the Suburban One Division. I had a mild case of acne, but so did everyone else.

Late one afternoon I was riding home from school in Steve Smolda's car. His car was our ticket to the world. Steve's 1983 light blue Chevy Malibu Classic had no working radio, but that doesn't mean we didn't rock 'n' roll in it. As we were speeding up Washington Lane, two Abington Township police cruisers with their lights flashing were coming in our direction. We assumed they were looking for us.

Steve drove that Malibu Classic like a stunt driver—always fast, always aggressive. Sometimes trash cans mysteriously jumped in front of the car, or Steve's Goodyears would find themselves a good distance off the road and rolling across some poor guy's lawn. It was entirely within reason to suspect that somebody had called the police on us.

Just before we reached the intersection of Washington Lane and George Road, the police cars turned left on George. We made a right, pulling in right behind them. And wouldn't you know it? They stopped right in front of my house.

Steve pulled into the driveway. The police parked out front along the curb. I got out of the car fast. So did Steve. I intercepted a large police officer who was walking quickly across the lawn toward our front door.

"What happened?" I asked the sergeant as we made our way to the front door together.

"We got a call about a medical emergency. A woman took a bad fall."

Waiting for us inside the house was my eight-year-old brother, Michael, who looked as if he'd seen a ghost. Behind Michael I could see a pair of legs splayed across the floor. They belonged to my forty-six-year-old mother, Carole. Our little Cairn Terrier, Danielle, was sitting guard by Mom's side.

"Kevin? Is that you?" Mom called out in a groggy voice.

"Yes," I answered. "What happened, Mom?"

"I don't know. I don't know why I'm on the floor. Why are the police here?"

Almost as soon as we arrived, an ambulance did too. The emergency medical technicians were inside so fast they may as well have fallen through the ceiling. When the EMTs moved closer to Mom, Danielle's hackles went up and she let out a low, protective growl.

"Can you take the dog away?" they asked.

"Good girl, Danielle," Mom said, appreciative of the love the little dog showed her.

I scooped Danielle up in my arms and put her inside an upstairs bedroom. When I came back downstairs to the kitchen, I finally asked Michael what he saw with Mom's fall.

"I heard a crash in the kitchen, then I came running up from downstairs. Mom was on the ground shaking and twitching, and her tongue was sticking out when I got to her. She didn't seem to know what was going on after she stopped shaking, so I called the police."

It was fast, brave thinking by Mike in a scary situation. How many eight-year-olds would react as well?

"That's mature thinking and reaction," the police sergeant told Michael. "Not a lot of children your age would have known what to do. I'm proud of you young man." As much of a hurry as the EMTs were in when they came into our house, they weren't in much of one to leave once they found Mom's vital signs to be stable. Still, there was no question we were going to the hospital for more tests. Before leaving the house, I left a note for my dad and older brother, Chris, on the kitchen table describing what had happened and where we would be.

Steve dropped Michael off at a friend's house down the street and promised to catch up with me later. I climbed into the ambulance with Mom and off we went.

When we got to Holy Redeemer Hospital, Mom changed into a gown before settling into her bed in a curtained-off area of the emergency room. She started to reminisce about her time working there as a nurse in the late 1960s. She quizzed everyone she saw about how long they'd worked there, and whether so and so was still around. There weren't many left from her time, and that made her a bit sad. I think she was hoping that some of her past colleagues whom she loved and trusted would take care of her.

As she was starting to mope, a familiar face peered around the privacy curtain that sectioned Mom off from the rest of the ER patients.

"Hi, Carole, are you feeling okay?"

"Oh Claudia, I don't really know," Mom answered.

It was Claudia Smolda, Steve's mom. Steve had gone home and told Claudia what had happened. Mom and Claudia were very tight, far tighter than we kids ever knew. Until then we didn't know how often the two women would talk on the telephone about us kids, sharing information, and consoling and counseling each other about motherhood. It was perfectly clear to me that day that there was a bond between Mom and Claudia that was just as strong as the one shared between their sons.

"Do you know what happened?" Claudia asked.

"I don't know. But I feel really hot," Mom answered.

Claudia moved up closer to Mom's head to have a more private discussion. Both women made a motion toward me by lifting and tilting their heads in the direction of the door. I took it as a hint that maybe I should take a walk. I went to the hospital cafeteria, put fifty cents in a vending machine, and bought a can of Coca-Cola.

When I came back, Mom and Claudia were finishing up. Claudia gave Mom a hug and told her to call when she got home. No sooner had Claudia walked out, Dad walked in. He gave Mom a kiss on the cheek and they talked privately for a moment. I took another walk and finished my Coke. When I came back, Mom was gone. She was off having tests done. She would spend the night. Dad drove me home.

The next day Mom came home from the hospital. There was no definitive answer as to what caused the seizure, so the doctors' best guess was that it was stress. I don't know that we were relieved that doctors didn't find something deeper, but we were sure glad to have Mom back home.

The same day Mom came home from Holy Redeemer, the same two Abington police officers who responded to Michael's emergency call paid a visit. I heard a knock on the door, opened it, and there they were.

"We were driving by and wanted to see if everything's okay."

I invited them in. Mom was thrilled to see them. They were relieved to see her. We were back inside the kitchen, just a couple of feet away from where Mom fell the day before. Naturally we made them some coffee.

"Hey where's that little guy who saved the day, the boy who called us on the phone?" the sergeant asked.

Mike was down the street playing with his friend Jonathan Grode. We called down there and told Mike to come home. When he came inside he looked stunned, no doubt worried by the sight of police cars parked outside the home for the second time in as many days. But when he saw Mom smiling, and the police sergeant slapped him five, he knew everything was okay.

"You're a hero," the sergeant told Michael, lifting my little brother's spirit at a time when he really needed it.

Michael beamed with pride. He should have. I was proud of him too.

Mom went back to work the next year, in 1986, when Chris went off to college at Villanova University on the Main Line of Philadelphia. Let me tell you about Villanova. Great school, damn expensive. With me going to college two years behind Chris, Mom wanted to help defray the high cost of our tuitions.

She took an overnight nursing job at Beaver College in Glenside, Pennsylvania, which has since been renamed Arcadia University. Mom really enjoyed the students. They were vivacious and mostly women. That was a real plus for her because of the male dominance in our home. But as anyone who's ever worked an overnight shift can tell you, it's brutal on the body. You never really adjust to the work schedule.

On top of the tough night and early morning hours, Mom would have to go two years seizure-free before she could legally drive a car again. This meant Dad, Chris, or I had to drop Mom off at the college at eleven p.m. and pick her up at seven the next morning. It was tough on everybody, but as Mom lovingly said, "I'd scrub floors if that's what it took to put you boys through college."

When a mom tells you that, how do you not honor her spirit and sacrifice? We grew up with the expectation that college wasn't something you aspired to, it was a given you were going to go. Mom grew up poor and put herself through Hunter College in New York City and St. Vincent's for nursing school. Dad, as I told you earlier, went to Georgetown.

Our parents worked so hard to get into and ultimately graduate from college with advanced degrees. They were good examples what higher education could lead to. Had we chosen not to go to college, or failed to excel once there, it would have been terribly disappointing to them. I just couldn't let that happen. For me, and I guess it's true for most children, there's hardly anything worse than letting your parents down.

"Kevin, I'm disappointed in you." I heard that a few times from my mom and dad. When I did, it crushed my spirit. I'm not sure who it hurt more, them or me. Conversely, there was nothing better than hearing your parents say, "I'm proud of you."

I wanted to make my parents proud of me whatever I did. I was a good student, not a great one. I got into several colleges of my choice, eventually choosing Purdue University in West Lafayette, Indiana. I received a partial athletic scholarship to play on the golf team. It was a chance to play major Division I sports at one of the country's better research institutions.

After signing my letter of intent in early 1988, I was content to enjoy the last few months of high school. It was not my proudest moment. I slacked off with my studies, driving my parents even crazier than Steve Smolda drove his car.

"He's reinventing senioritis," my guidance counselor, Jeffery Marmon, told my mother.

That was Mr. Marmon's general observation and an accurate one. A more detailed accounting of my class credits revealed something else.

"If you don't pass every class second semester, you won't graduate!" Mr. Marmon warned me behind the closed door of his office with his eyes bulging out of his head. "Most people graduate with several credits to spare, but you're right on the line."

I got the message and turned it around. Well, "hung in there" is a probably a better description. I walked with my class at graduation and spoke during the commencement ceremony with a single credit to spare.

When my parents put me on a plane bound for Purdue in August 1988, my mom cried as I hugged her goodbye. She was relieved and proud to see me start college, but sad to see me go. Purdue was a lot farther away than Chris's forty-five-minute drive to Villanova. It was too great a distance for semi-regular trips home or visits to campus from Mom and Dad.

For a couple of years we didn't know the what led to the first seizure that caused Mom to topple in the kitchen that day in 1985. Nor did we know what led to the occasional seizure that followed. But when the seizures started happening with increased frequency, it was clear there was something else going on in addition to whatever "stress" Mom was feeling. I kept tabs from far away by way of collect calls.

I knew it was trouble when my dad called me my sophomore year, 1990. "Mom's sick," he said, "she's going to need brain surgery. Why don't you come home for a couple of days."

I flew home to Pennsylvania the next day. I walked into the house and found Mom doing laundry downstairs with our Cairn Terrier Danielle lying on top of a pile of dirties. She would have surgery the following day. I told her I loved her and hugged her. Then I asked, "Are you worried, Mom?"

"If it were anywhere else on my body I don't think I would be. *But it's my head*," she said before bursting into tears.

It was the word *head* and how she said *head* that made the difference. She was just really struggling with the fact that someone was going to saw into her skull. I was feeling the same angst; I just couldn't quite express it in words. Mom did it for both of us.

"I don't know if I'll come out the same. I'm walking into the hospital, but I don't know if I'm walking out," Mom said worriedly.

Turns out she did walk out. The surgery went well, but the pathology on the mass removed from her parietal lobe was not good news. It was a low-grade cancerous tumor. Despite the news that the cancer would likely be terminal over time, we had several more good months with Mom after her surgery. With the mass no longer pressing down on the area of her brain that controlled her emotions, her mood and motor skills greatly improved. But it wouldn't last. The seizures returned and so did her struggles with depression. Another MRI revealed the tumor was back and it was bigger.

On top of Mom's deteriorating health, our family moved from Meadowbrook, Pennsylvania, to Ledyard, Connecticut, as Dad took a new job. We were strangers in a strange land, having to relearn the entire health care landscape. Mom had a second brain surgery in 1991. It left her paralyzed on her left side. The pathology on the tumor confirmed what we feared most. The cancer had worsened from stage two to stage four. By now we were pretty much counting the time we had left as we tried to keep Mom comfortable.

Dad really struggled. He was working a demanding job in a new place. His wife was dying, and she needed almost constant care. His oldest son, Chris, was busy trying to get his working life started after graduation. I was away at college. Michael was a little too young at fourteen to be trusted with major responsibility.

In August 1991, I got another urgent call at school from my dad. I had just finished up a summer session, which I needed to catch up on credits. I had a few days before the start of the fall semester and my senior year. It was nice to have a break from my studies. I used the extra time to relax and to get my golf game back into shape for the fall season.

Dad asked me to drive home right away. With school restarting in less than a week, I thought it would be best to fly. Dad insisted I drive. He said there were more details that he'd share once I arrived. My wife, Jean, then my girlfriend, was with me when I got the call. She offered to ride back with me on the sixteen-hour drive to the new family home in Connecticut and stay for a couple of days to help with Mom. Dad said it was best that I come alone.

I hadn't seen Mom since Christmas break. What I saw when I walked in the door was really tough. She looked so different. It had been a little more than eight months, but it looked as if she'd aged eight years. The color consistency in her face was splotchy—the obvious effects of the cancer and the chemo. She saw in my face the same fear and sadness I saw in hers. Mom was mostly bedridden at this point. But she managed to smile for me, and with my help she stood up and hugged me with the half of her body that still worked.

It wasn't long before I sat down with Dad. "I need you to take some time off from college," he said, "maybe a semester, maybe a year. I really need your help and so does Mom."

The reason Dad asked me to drive home was so my car wouldn't be left behind at school. He knew I wasn't going back, but he didn't want to tip me off. He said it was one of the toughest things he ever had to ask of anyone. "It was your senior year, I knew I was asking a lot of you."

My wonderful college life was about to be disrupted. I'd have to leave my teammates, I wouldn't graduate with my friends, and I'd be away from my new girlfriend and future wife for months. I picked up the phone and called Jean at her parents' home in Palos Heights, Illinois. That call was probably as tough as the one Dad made to me two days before.

"I won't be back for at least a semester, maybe even a year," I told her.

"Oh my God," Jean said. "How bad is it?"

"It's really bad. She's really deteriorated."

"Oh my God. I'm so sorry."

I wasn't just stunned and sad, I was angry. Why couldn't Dad, Chris, and Michael figure out a way to divide the responsibility among them? I mean they were already *there*. I had a life 900 miles away—or at least I did the day before.

There was something else. I was worried about my relationship with Jean. We'd been dating for little more than a year and our relationship was solid. But a year away from your significant other in the college years is an eternity. There were plenty of examples of relationships around us that failed similar time and distance.

Jean couldn't have been more loving and encouraging about what was going to be a difficult stretch.

"Just take good care of your mom. It's going to be hard for you and your mom and for me, but you'll be better for doing this. I'm not going anywhere. I understand why you're angry. Something good will eventually come out of this," she said while sobbing.

After a couple of hours with proper reflection, I thought about the courage it took for my dad to ask me for help, and the trust he and Mom had in me to handle the responsibility. As far as the resentment I held toward my dad and brothers? It was very real and ultimately very misguided.

The reality was Dad and Chris had just started new jobs and they needed to protect them. Dad was helping Mom very early in the morning, turning her over to an in-home nurse before going off to work, rushing home to relieve the nurse, make dinner, and then take care of Mom the rest of the night. If that sounds difficult, I don't think you're even halfway there to truly understanding how hard and exhausting it really was. Here was a man whose wife was dying, his heart was breaking, and he was just trying to make an honest living while keeping the ship afloat. This was martyrdom.

Then there were my brothers. Chris had been living in Hilton Head, South Carolina, after graduating from Villanova in 1990. He moved up North to help my parents with the move from Pennsylvania to Ledyard, Connecticut. He had already done far more for Mom and Dad than I knew, was helping out with Mom and around the house when he could, all the while working a demanding schedule with a defense contractor in New London.

Michael had just turned fourteen. He was the new kid in a new town. That's tough under any circumstances. His was a childhood I wouldn't wish on anyone. My siblings had been through enough already. The whole family was suffering, except for me. Now it was my turn to make sacrifices too.

I thought about Jean and how she said she'd wait for me. I thought about Mom and all the times she took care of me when I was sick, all the sacrifices she made for me and my brothers, and her offer to "scrub floors if that's what it took to put you boys through college."

That's when I knew I had to do it. It wasn't just a responsibility, it was an *honor* to take care of Mom. It was a *privilege* to return to her a fraction of the love and care she'd bestowed upon me every day of my *life*. College could wait. Mom couldn't. In the end it was an easy decision to make.

"Yeah, Dad, I'm in," I told him before I said goodnight.

It was a trying late summer and early fall. I woke up with Mom in the morning and took care of her during the day. Dad would relieve me at night. I had a lot of good talks with Mom by her bedside. We talked about life, death, life after death, and I think she really enjoyed the time. I know I did. We did more talking in four weeks than we did my entire life.

With the tumor growing inside of Mom's head, her eyesight was deteriorating. Not able to read, I read for her. No longer able to go to the bathroom by herself, I took her in. Now Mom was a very private person so I'll spare you the details. But I'm sure you can imagine how difficult it was for a son to care for his mother how she once cared for him. If there's anything more humbling than that, I don't know what it is. Mothers don't give up their modesty easily.

My younger brother, Michael, had just a modest helping of Mom at her motherly best. For the most part she wasn't able to shower him with the love and attention that Chris and I, and even our friends, took as givens. But given what was and wasn't given to Michael as a boy, he took his hard life like a man. The cancer caused Mom so much pain, and the mood-altering effects of the medication and chemotherapy robbed Michael of the mother that Chris and I knew. What's more, in its totality Chris and I were away at college during some of Mom's most difficult moments, leaving Michael to shoulder more stress than any young adolescent should ever have to.

Mom died on September 26, 1991, just a few hours after my parents' twenty-fifth wedding anniversary. Her loss was felt on so many levels. Dad was a widower at fifty-one, and Michael was motherless at fourteen. That made for a lonely house in Ledyard, Connecticut, for a long time.

SEVENTEEN

My New Mom and the Greatest Love Story Ever

Bob Walsh and Mary McGrattan, March 2013

"Hello, Dolly," Dad said, answering a call while lying on his bed at the Holiday Inn Express in room 106 after a long day of fishing.

It was Mary, his second wife.

Now I know my dad loved my mom, Carole, very much. There's probably not a day that goes by that he doesn't think about her. But the story of how Dad met Mary—or "When Dad Met Mary" as we call it in our family— is the greatest love story ever. I'll fight anyone who says differently.

Mom's death led to upheaval. I went back to school in Indiana. Chris had moved on from the defense contractor job and was now working for Merrill Lynch in Jacksonville, Florida. What's more, Chris took the family Golden Retriever, Susie, with him. That left Dad and Michael home alone. The house in Ledyard is big, about 3,000 square feet. That's a lot of space for just two people, especially those who don't talk much to begin with. The silence was painful.

"Dad was always trying to organize activities for us to do together," Mike would explain to me years later. Dad and Mike's time together, just the two of them, was a bit of a mystery. Chris and I were out of the house at this point. We always wondered how Dad and Mike adjusted.

"We golfed a bit and went bowling. We both got bowling balls. I learned that Dad was a pretty good bowler in his younger years and still had some skill," Mike told me.

What skills Dad had in bowling, he lacked in domesticity.

"I do remember for a while in the beginning we sent the laundry to a laundromat for wash and fold service. I asked Dad to stop doing that because our white shirts came back with orange spots. We figured out how to do our own laundry, and I treated the dryer as my own personal dresser. I would pull my clothes from the dryer and get dressed in the laundry room every day. This bad habit continues and drives my wife nuts."

Dinners were simple. "A lot of canned stuff," Mike remembers. "If anything it may have helped me because I was a little overweight at that time. Going from Mom's food and cookies and spoiling us with any junk food we wanted, to eating tuna fish out of a can, will trim you down."

Mike and Dad are not picky eaters, so it didn't make much difference. They ate for sustenance, not joy. With many a meal they shared, hardly a word was spoken. But they were together, and they had each other. These were good bonding times, but eventually an adolescent is going to need his friends, and a man is going to need a woman.

Dad grieved Mom's death for a good year or so. Then one day, when Chris and I were back home for the holidays, he gathered us sons together in the basement of his Ledyard home.

"You boys know I loved your mother very much," he said painfully through the tears. "I still have a lot of life left, and there may come a time that I have another woman in my life. I'm too young to be alone for the rest of my life."

It was honorable, courageous, and awkward. He probably thought we might not want to see him with another woman. I admired him for the husband he was to Mom and the father he's always been to us. When I told him how proud I was of him, I returned the magic words he said to me so many times when my heart needed a lift, or when I had truly done something well. Then I sought to lighten the mood of the difficult moment with humor.

"Well, Dad, if you want to go trolling for chicks, we can do that right now. I'll take you out."

"Oh, no. Oh no, no, no, no. I can't go out on the bar scene, that's not me. And I have conditions. I want to get married again, but I don't want to raise another family—I'm too old. I want to get married in the Catholic Church. So whoever she is, she can't be divorced. She has to have never been married, or be widowed with grown children."

"Uh, Dad, you know, I think God is going to make an exception on this one. There's just not a lot of what you're looking for at your age. You've narrowed the pool from this [stretching my hands about a foot apart] to this [narrowing my hands to an inch]. You may need to expand the options," I suggested.

It's weird thinking about your dad on the dating scene. You fear the possibility of seeing your old man engaging in public displays of lovey dovey. Fortunately we didn't see any of that—or at least I didn't. You also hear people talk about your dad in ways you've never heard before.

"Your dad is very handsome," a few women friends of the family told me. I mean that's great, but you don't want your friends' moms digging on your dad.

To help with the constant loneliness, Dad and Michael decided to get a new dog. Combing through the classifieds in the newspaper, they found a Dalmatian breeder in Danielson, Connecticut. They moved fast and bought a dog with spots on the spot. Daisy moved in and brought a cheer and a female presence to a place that sorely needed it.

Not only did Daisy help life inside the house, she did so elsewhere. "She was a chick magnet," Dad says.

Dad would take Daisy to downtown Mystic for walks and ultimately start a parade. Young girls, twenty-somethings, mothers, and grandmothers came rushing out of stores, wanting a closer look and a chance to pet the cute puppy. It also gave Dad the opportunity to chat those ladies up. Here's the million-dollar question: was Dad using the dog as a tool?

"No, no, no," Dad insists. "I didn't use her to pick up chicks."

If Dad didn't, Mike certainly tried. There were girls his age in the neighborhood. "They were interested in seeing Daisy, and I was interested in seeing them," he admits.

But a dog could only do so much. As far as sealing the deal, we're fairly sure Mike came up short. Mike picked up the social slack with some neighborhood pals, Anthony and Tommy. Nobody called Anthony *Anthony*, except his mother and our stepmother. It was *Tone*—one syllable, not two.

Mike, Tone, and Tommy spent a lot of their formative years cruising around the neighborhood on their bikes and playing street hockey and baseball. Pretty wild, huh? Actually it was, eventually.

Mike and Tommy went through an experimental phase that most young men do. "Smoking cigarettes, chewing tobacco, and shooting shit with our BB guns," Mike confesses with hardly a regret. "I think you and Chris had broken Dad in pretty well because he was less strict at this point. He had been through some difficult times. His edge was not what it used to be. Fortunately I did not feel the need to take advantage of the circumstances too much. I suppose a combination of good, well-raised friends and luck kept me out of drugs and heavy drinking. I also did not want to give him any more garbage to deal with. I had a generally great time, and for the most part stayed out of trouble."

I met a couple of the women Dad went on a few dates with. They were nice enough, but ultimately those relationships didn't really go anywhere. Not that I could be much of a judge though. It wasn't long before I was out of the house for good. The same was true for Chris. Mike? Different story.

"Yeah, Dad dated and I did not love it in the beginning," Mike told me years later. "I have seen plenty of TV shows and movies where kids lose a parent, the survivor dates someone, and the kids resent the person no matter what. That was not the case here. I did not expect Dad to be alone for an extended period in his life.

Instead I was worried about him jumping into something with the wrong person. The exception was Mrs. McGrattan. She did not need Dad. She was independent, successful, and had a full life in my eyes as a sixteen-year-old at the time. In that way I felt better about her, like the appreciation and interest she had for Dad was more true."

In early 1995, a call in the middle of the night woke Jean and me up. It was 3 a.m. Guam time. The Territory of Guam is American soil on the other side of the International Date Line. It is sixteen hours ahead of the East Coast. Knowing our families would never remember the time difference, Jean and I gave them printed time charts that would do the time conversion for them. Nobody ever bothered to look at them. They called whenever they pleased, feigning ignorance when they discovered they had woken us up.

It was expensive to call internationally back then, almost two dollars a minute. When our families said, "You want to call us back when you wake up?"

We'd quickly say, "No we'll talk right now!" That way they paid for it.

Any time the phone rings at 3 a.m. you assume it's bad family news. Not this time.

"Hey, Kevin," Dad announced excitedly into the receiver. "Guess what? I'm engaged."

"What? Really? I didn't even know you had a girlfriend. Anyone I know?"

"Yes it is. You've met her before. Do you remember Mary McGrattan, the former mayor of Ledyard?"

"Of course."

"It's her."

Dad and Mary's story is as improbable as it is wonderful.

I had met Mary when I was with my mom and dad a week before Mom died in September 1991. We were at Ledyard City

Hall. Mom had to sign some power of attorney documents and get them notarized before we took her off the steroidal medication that was keeping her brain tumor in check. Once we did that, the cancer was expected to and eventually did grow very rapidly.

Mary is a nurse, just like Mom was. Mary was also the mayor of Ledyard and a notary public at the time of Mom's illness. She was very kind to Mom the day we all met with her. She made sure my mother knew exactly what she was signing before Mary affixed her notary seal.

A couple of years later, Dad met Mary at a work-related cocktail party. She didn't remember him, but he most certainly remembered her. Mary had graduated from town mayor to Connecticut state representative. Dad, who worked for Pfizer Pharmaceuticals, was assigned to lobby lawmakers about why his company charged what it did for the medicines it made. This was a time when pharmaceuticals were subject to relentless PR pressure about their pricing and profits. That's "When Dad met Mary."

Mary McGrattan was widowed, the mother of six adult children. She is a good Catholic and exactly what Dad was looking for. They married in June 1995. I flew five legs and thirty-three hours from Guam to Connecticut to be there. The worst leg of the trip was from LA to Cleveland. A female passenger next to me slept sideways in her seat, perching her butt cheeks on my armrest, and farting in my face the entire time on the redeye connection. Few things reinforce memory more than smell. But that's one I'd rather forget.

I introduced myself to my future stepmother when she picked me up at TF Green Airport in Providence, Rhode Island. The next day I introduced her and Dad as man and wife at their wedding in New London, Connecticut. Not a lot of sons get to do that.

Mary moved into our family home soon after the wedding. There are still pictures of my Mom around the house, but my stepmother has certainly added her touches, all of which are in very good taste. I call her Mary. My children and the rest of the twenty grandchildren between her and my dad call her Ni Ni. My brother, Michael, still calls her Mrs. McGrattan after all these years. Old habits are hard to break, and Mary is just fine with it.

Like my mom, Mary has no interest in fishing. But she understands what it does for my dad. When he goes down to his basement workshop to build rods and tie flies, she retires to her sewing room or reads by the fireplace. And when Dad goes on his fishing trips, she'll often visit her adult children who are spread around the country just like us. Whenever Dad and Mary are apart, they check in by phone each night.

"Good night, Dolly," he said while pressing end call on his iPhone.

With that, he turned off the light on his nightstand. "Good night, Kevin."

"Good night, Dad."

EIGHTEEN

The Perfect Catch

The Perfect Catch. Paul Jacob holding steelhead with Bob Walsh, Western New York, November 2012

The next day's wakeup call came much easier than the first. First of all, no one was hung over. Second, we were all reasonably well rested. I started the truck a few minutes early to warm up the cab and defrost the windows. It was 28 degrees at 4 a.m. We threw our gear in the back and climbed in up front. As soon as I started driving out of the Holiday Inn Express parking lot, a warning light on the dashboard flicked on.

"You gotta be effin' kidding me!" I screamed, causing Dad to flinch.

It was a warning about low tire pressure. Without feeling a wobble, I was pretty sure a nail, or something else sharp, was stuck in a tire causing a slow leak. I pulled over to check, and there it was—a large screw right smack in the center of the front right tire. I've had a few of those in my day and I know it's better to keep them in, rather than pull them out. The obstruction stanches the deflation.

The damaged tire didn't look all that bad, and there was no hissing sound. I figured we could safely drive to the river. The fix could wait, the fish couldn't. We made it to the meeting place without incident.

Paul and Norm were sitting on the bumper of Paul's Ford Explorer. A wood dowel held the back hatch open. They were tying thin tapered tippet line onto heavier leaders, sliding beads onto tippet, and then tying hooks just below the beads. They were ready to go and so were we.

Norm would take Chris and me down the trail and to the river. We were hoping to fish the same spot in river, but on the other side. Paul planned to take Dad and Mike to a different river with private access about twenty minutes away. We said goodbye to Mike, Dad and Paul, and Norm, Chris, and I started the slow walk downhill.

It was a much trickier walk in than the day before. There was cloud cover, which kept the light of the moon out of the picture.

We followed the light of our headlamps along the narrow path to the water's edge. We walked along the relatively flat riverbank for about a hundred yards, holding our fly rods backwards. It's always wise to do this because forward pointing rod tips get snagged on trees, brush, and saplings. I've seen rod tips snap when a fisherman takes a tumble forward. It's happened to me, and it absolutely ruins your day.

When the trail turned rugged with a slope that was slippery even with our corkers on, Norm decided a walk in the water was better than a walk on land.

We used the slippery slope to our advantage to enter the water. We sat down and slid in, feeling the water squeeze the edges of our waders like tight jeans on wash day. We followed closely behind Norm staying as near to the edge of the riverbank as we could. It was so dark we could hardly see the water even though we were in it.

"Okay, watch here," Norm said, shining a flashlight on a spot and pointing with his finger. "There's a big rock underwater."

Chris altered his moving motion from a march to a kick and slide. When he got to the spot that Norm alerted us to, he tapped the rock with the toe of his left boot. He stopped for a moment and traced half the circumference of the rock with the inside and outside edge of his boot. It was big enough that had you walked into it without warning, you likely would have taken a wet fall. So far we're all intact and dry.

A minute later, fifty yards downstream, another heads up.

"Chris, Kevin? There's a deep hole right here. Just slide your feet through carefully," Norm advised.

When we got to the dip in the river, we shuffled our feet carefully. I even grabbed onto a bush that extended out. Like the rock we just passed, had we not known the hole was there, the sudden change of terrain would have likely caused a stumble. We kept following Norm, our shepherd.

After about ten minutes of wading, we pulled ourselves out of the water and onto the bank. We took our backpacks off and put them on higher ground. As we were doing that, two lights flicked on from the other side of the river. "Good morning," a familiar voice boomed.

"Is that you, Norm, with the brothers?"

"Yes, it is," Norm answered. "It's Bob and Jack right?"

"Yes," the older gentlemen answered.

"Hey, Norm, I just want to thank you again for the other day," Bob said.

"Oh you got it. It's no big deal. That's what we do for each other," Norm replied.

Actually it was a big deal. A couple of days earlier Bob had latched onto a big fish. The fish made a massive run downstream and Bob went chasing after him. During the chase he lost his footing and went for a most uncomfortable swim downstream. "He had a look of death on his face," Norm told Chris and me later.

Norm stepped out into the deeper water and snagged Bob by the arm and back of his fishing vest. He got the distressed fisherman over to the riverbank, minus his fly rod, which was floating downstream. As Norm got Bob settled and calmed down, another fisherman came marching up against the current with Bob's rod in hand. Cold, wet, and exhausted, Bob spent the rest of the day recovering under blankets inside his camper at the top of the hill.

"I'm not chasing any more fish downriver, Norm," Bob said. "I'm too old for that shit."

"Well if you change your mind and it happens again, I'll fish you out again," Norm said with a laugh that made everyone else laugh too.

Norm didn't belabor the hero part, because that's not what true fishermen do. You help people in need and hope the karma of the good deed is returned sometime, somewhere down the river.

Anyone who's spent any appreciable time on water, or in it, knows it's not a question of *if*, but *when* your time of need will come.

Our time of fishing wouldn't come for another forty-five minutes or so, so we parked ourselves on the bank and BS'd to while the time away. Somewhere in the course of our wait Chris ripped a tremendous fart, which echoed through his waders and was boosted by the acoustics of the semi-canyon we were in.

"Yo, is that from the beef on weck sandwich? Or is that the two-day leftover from your big beer night with Mike?" I asked.

"I dunno, but check this out. Have you seen the Breaking the Barrier video?" Chris asked while pulling his iPhone out of his pocket.

Chris dialed up YouTube and hit play on a video in which the actors in the skit are a boyfriend and girlfriend who've reached the point in their relationship where they're now comfortable farting around each other. The genius of the comedy is that *it's the girl* who takes exceptional liberty with her newfound farting freedom. When she catches a fart in her hand and cupped it over her boyfriend's nose announcing, "Cup of cheese!" we thought about when we cut the cheese and did the same thing to each other as kids. I laughed so hard I almost fell into the river.

"Hey! Hey! Whaddaya watching girly videos over there?" either Bob or Jack wanted to know.

"Not quite," I answered. "There's a pretty girl involved, but she's not naked. She farts a lot."

A long silence then, "Don't let that interfere with your fishing now."

As we squatted on our spot, the other half of our family was pulling into the private driveway of one of Paul's friends. Michael described the scene to us later when we compared notes about our fishing day.

It was a driveway only in the sense that there were cars parked on worn grass alongside a newer log cabin–style home. There was a barn to the left of the home and open space behind each. If you were ever looking for a place to get away from it all, this was the place.

Because the land was private, there was no need to get out in the water early to secure a spot. When it was time to fish, they'd have the place all to themselves. Paul and Dad kicked back in the front seat sharing conversation and morning coffee in Styrofoam cups. They talked about fishing and the different spots on the property to fish while waiting for the sun to rise. Dad left Mike in the back seat snoring away—and happy to be doing so. He would time his rise with that of the sun.

When the sun finally rose, Chris and I stood up on the riverbank, adjusted our waders, and took a good look at the now-familiar rapids. We pretty much knew where to cast, and we were especially happy to be fishing on the forehand. The forehand motion was just so much more natural, accurate, and painless. It didn't take long for the fish to strike.

"Kevin, see that inside edge of the feeder line?" Norm asked while pointing to a narrow swath of bubbles no more than twenty feet in front of me. "Try that and let it drift down toward the bend."

I cast upstream, mended the line, and pointed the rod tip at the strike indicator as it drifted from my left to my right. By the time the egg reached thirty feet to my right and almost directly sideways from my right hip, the orange float sank underneath a hanging tree.

"Set!" Norm announced.

Oh, I set the hook all right. The fish took off running in the direction of the nervous water. It made a nervous jump in the middle of the ripples, before splashing down and heading downriver in the direction from which it came. By the feel in my hands I could tell it was not a big fish, but it was a sporty one. It made a couple more jumps and jukes before giving up the fight. Landing the fish that strikes first is significant. It's a tone setter, similar to the first hole in a round of golf. After three or four minutes, it was all over.

The fish in Norm's net was a decent-sized chromer, fishing-speak for a steelhead that looks chrome-colored. When steelheads leave the lake to start their spawning journey upriver, they're all shiny. The longer a fish stays in the river, the darker it becomes with different hues. Based on this fish's ultra silvery shine, it hadn't been in the river long. It was a golden start.

Chris, upriver to my left, caught a fish right after me. It was a six-pound steelhead with more colors of the rainbow. It was shaping up to be a good day. Our arms certainly felt better from a night's rest, and because we were casting on the forehand we felt as if we could do this forever.

More fish came for both of us, including a monster steelhead that Chris had on the line for almost a half hour.

"He was heavy. It was like pulling in a log," Chris said.

The big fish hunkered down, ran downstream several times, and showed a profound willingness to not be caught. I had to reel my line in several times so it wouldn't get tangled with Chris's line that was zigzagging through my zone and that of Bob and Jack's across the river. Just when it looked as if it was going to end positively, the taut line went soft and slack. Chris just stood there in knee-deep water with an amused look on his face.

"You're taking that a lot better than I would," I told him.

"What can you do?" he asked, more in the form of a statement than a question.

What couldn't Mike and Dad do where they were? It was hard to say whether they were on fish, or fish were on them.

"Mike was into a nice five-pound brown trout moments after he started fishing," Dad recounted their day later. "It was heaven to watch Mike land this fish."

Heaven wasn't just the fishing. It was the scenery where Dad and Mike were. This was much different from the other river by the dam that cut through a gorge. Dad and Mike were fishing in the middle of open land. The river was much less crowded with trees, but surrounded by tall grasses that had browned in the cooler fall months. A red barn with a black, beveled roof, and a single white silo with a silver top standing next to it added to the idyllic setting.

"The brook where we fished was really beautiful, really peaceful," Mike described to us.

When Mike wasn't focused on the water in front of him, he could see a most interested spectator off to the side. "Dad really liked watching me fish. I don't know what it was, but he was looking at me a lot."

"I watched Mike cast, and he did well. I think he might yet become a devoted fly fisherman," Dad said.

Dad's pride only swelled as he saw his son pull another *eight* fish out of the same pool.

"He really looked like he was enjoying himself," Dad said. "Fortunately he had no more urgent phone calls from his office and I think he began to sense the quietness of fly fishing."

The peace that eluded Mike the first two days of the trip found him on the last day of fishing. Mike's peace gave Dad the same. The bite wasn't as excellent where Dad was in the river, but it was still pretty good. Dad reeled a couple in.

Dad, Mike, and Paul broke for lunch right around the same time we did. They went to the old reliable gas station/deli where Paul practically owns stock. Norm, Chris, and I went to a newly redone bar and grill. As different as our places to eat were, the diners were remarkably the same—lots of hunters and fishermen.

The waitress at our restaurant was named Tricia. She had arm tattoos and a pierced tongue. She kept getting tongue tied when trying to give us the specials. She was cute and helpful, though we didn't take her up on the specials. Norm was just glad to be eating somewhere other than the gas station/deli.

"After a month of eating there every single day, I need a break," he said as he tore into a Reuben sandwich.

I had pulled pork. Chris had the house hamburger. The food was really good.

Mike was enjoying a roast beef sandwich while Dad munched on ham and cheese. Paul was curling his spoon in some chicken broth–based soup. At the next table over, several hunters were talking about the geese they bagged that morning and how they were going to prepare the geese for dinner.

"I didn't enjoy that part of their conversation, but I always like to hear a different accent," Mike says. "I envied those guys because it seemed like they had so much free time that they could hunt just about any day they wanted to."

When lunch was done Norm and Paul hooked up by phone. Paul would be taking Mike and Dad a little farther downriver by a bridge. Norm gave Chris and me the option to go back and fish where we did in the morning, or try new water.

"Let's try new water," I told him. "We pretty much know what that other place brings. A change of scenery would be nice."

To that Norm and Chris were agreeable. We ended up at a place a mile farther downriver and closer to Lake Ontario. From the top of the cliff the water below looked much calmer than where we had been, and the river was certainly wider. There was a sandy island in the middle of the river, which not only looked lovely but also produced a gentle bend to the right. We decided to give it a shot.

The hike down from the bluff took about ten minutes. As we waded into the water on the other side of the island, I quickly realized that the water was not as calm as it looked from above. It was also deeper than the previous place. The combination of faster, deeper water meant we had to keep our hands higher and we had to brace against the current by leaning into it. The extra lift and lean put a lot of pressure on my chronic back condition. On the other hand, the new water offered plenty of room to cast, which is half the fun of fly fishing.

I had four fish on, but lost them all. Chris was doing well. With casting at a higher premium here, Chris was really in his element and the fish followed. He brought in a couple of steelheads and a brown in short order. The deeper, faster water also gave us a chance to fish with different patterns and retrievals. Switching from eggs to streamers gave us more to do with stripping the line. More stripping, like more casting, is more fun.

Under a steel grate bridge Michael was stripping an egg pattern across a ripple near a stanchion. Bam! A steelhead hit. Bam! It happened again on the next cast. Two casts, two fish caught. Paul didn't just put Mike on fish, he put him on a honey pot that Dad and Mike were happy to share stories about when we met up later. There was another fisherman on the riverbank trying to sample the glory with marshmallows for bait. He didn't catch a thing with the marshmallows, but insisted it was fishing magic that Mike should try.

"No thanks, I think I'm good," Mike said waving him off.

Cars were driving across the steel grate overhead, which was rough on the ears, but not on the fishing. Mike said he kept pulling them out and Paul kept netting them. One particular catch caught the attention of a heavy-set Eastern European woman who asked for the fish. Mike didn't know what to say.

"No," Paul answered.

She persisted. Paul would have none of it, staying true to his catch and release way of life. Eventually the woman moved on, and Mike kept catching fish.

Dad wasn't having quite the same bonanza up the river, but he couldn't get enough of watching Mike do his thing. He was equally impressed with Paul's ability to put Mike on fish. Before putting Mike in the water under the bridge, Paul checked out the water for just a minute or so while Mike and Dad waited in the car. Paul said the fishing would be good. He was wrong. The fishing was great.

Chris and I only wished we had it as great as Mike and Dad on the second day, but we still had it pretty good. With time winding down on the afternoon, Norm suggested we move farther down the river, which wound to our right before winding back to the left again. I welcomed the walk because it loosened up my stiffening back. Plus, I hoped a new spot would bring better luck.

We trudged over some mud flats where the carcasses of King Salmon were rotting after a run earlier in the fall when the water was higher. The smell was awful and the sight grisly, but this is part and parcel of the life cycle of salmon, which left Lake Ontario to swim up the tributary to spawn in the same place where they had been born.

The sight of the dead fish reminded me of our original mission on this trip—going back to our roots. The difference was, we did it for fun, friendship, and family. These fish died for having done it.

The new spot featured the view of a small, poorly conditioned house about thirty yards off the riverbank on the other side. There was a hammock in front, a couple of tents off to the side, and "No Trespassing" signs posted on every tree along the river's edge. It was a clear message that we weren't welcome to fish on that side.

Large, empty wine bottles hung from the trees with string tied around their necks. I wasn't sure if that was a message to poachers or a shooting gallery for the property owner. Either way I found hanging wine bottles odd. I would have expected beer cans or bottles before wine, but who knows? There were a lot of hanging empties, which told me whoever spends time there drinks like a fish when they're not catching them.

The fishing had slowed and Chris and I were tiring fast. Two straight days of hard fishing really took a toll on us. We turned to Norm and said we were happy to call it a day. He had no complaint and led us back to the spot we came from. We would wait at my truck for Dad, Mike, and Paul to come to us when they were done. It would be about an hour because Mike and Dad had locked in on some exceptional late afternoon fishing.

"About twenty minutes before four the fish really made a run," Dad told us later.

He told us how he was standing in water that was calm and about waist deep. He cast a sparsely tied black and gray wooly bugger into a stretch of faster water about thirty feet away. He threw the fly to ten o'clock and let it drift to twelve. If there was no strike before twelve, he'd start a slow strip with the fly back toward him. No strike indicator here, just feel. This was old fashioned fishing—perfect for Dad. The spot turned golden with Dad pulling in three fish in fifteen minutes—two browns and a steelhead.

Mike had seen Dad's late afternoon charge and took a break from his fishing to watch his father at work on the water. The sight of Dad pulling them in made Mike a happy son. Dad's no showoff, but something happened that sent a spark through the water.

At about 4:15 Dad cast back to the ten o'clock spot. The fly never made it to twelve on the drift before a fish blew up the water. It was clear this was the fish of the trip.

"Oh, you could tell by the wake the fish created in the water that it was *big*," Dad relates.

Paul, who was splitting the distance between Dad and Mike heard the splashing from the strike and early fight. He headed over right away with a glow on his face.

"Now, Bob, remember that's four-pound test you have on the line," he said with a warning tone.

"Paul was really excited. I could tell he really wanted to catch that fish," Dad says. "I did too. I knew it was big."

The fish zigzagged across the pool, made a run *upriver*—which almost never happens, unless it's a really big one. Knowing he had light line on, Dad kept the rod tip up, while making sure not to horse the fish.

"Bob, it's four-pound test," Paul said again.

That was twice now that Paul reminded Dad to take it easy. The redundancy and urgency in Paul's voice made Dad lock in even more. He didn't want the fish to get away; it would have been so disappointing for him and Paul, and Mike too who was now moving closer with a camera in hand.

With a good hook set and a lot of open water, Dad knew that if he was patient he could wait the fish out. He didn't do much reeling in. He just let the fish swim around with the line that was already out. And swim the fish did. Hard. Slicing through the water and making waves. "Ziiiinnnggg" went the reel, letting out more line—at a price.

As the fish pulled line out and taxed Dad's weathered hands, it was taxing itself too. That extra line was extra weight on its body, compounded by the tension from the drag set on the reel. Holding the rod high gave Dad the upper hand, ensuring that for every zig and zag the fish did, there was a responding flex in the rod, which absorbed the fish's power and efforts to spit the hook.

After four more runs, it was clear the fish was tiring. Slowly, but deliberately, Dad reeled in. Paul moved closer to the line, sliding his feet gently along the river bottom, not wanting to spook the fish and prompting another run. Dad held still, keeping tension on the line as Paul grabbed the top of the leader with his left hand, sliding it down closer to the fish. With a good squeeze of the line, Paul took over control of the fish.

With the line in his left hand, and the net in his right, Paul scooped up an absolutely gorgeous thirty-inch steelhead chromer.

"That's a beautiful fish, Bob," he said to Dad who was grinning like a child on Christmas.

"Oh, Dad, that's a beauty. That's a really nice fish," Mike said as he inched closer with the camera and was snapping away. Mike was so proud. He was happy for Dad to catch what was the prize catch of the trip, and one of the best fish in his life.

Dad said little, but his face said it all. He had the buzz. He was beaming. He gave so much to make this trip happen. It was as if the gift was returned to him, a living lifetime achievement award being held in his hands.

"Dad, stand next to Paul," Mike instructed.

Tired from the fight and wanting Paul to share in the moment, Dad handed the fish over to his faithful guide. Paul turned the fish on its side and admired its size, symmetry, spots, and just a hint of pink coloring. Paul was grinning, Dad was glowing, and Mike wanted the picture to capture the essence of what just happened.

Paul held the fish up and extended his arms out. Dad stepped into frame, put his right hand on the small of Paul's back and held his fly rod off to the side in his left hand. With little left to do, Mike took the perfect picture of two men who together made the perfect catch.

NINETEEN

Tell Your Sons to Go Fishing

From left: Michael, Kevin, Chris, and Bob Walsh at Alex's Place, Batavia, New York, 2012

There was a lot to celebrate that night, the final night of the trip. Naturally we would do it with food and drink.

"I'm gonna have a beer," Dad announced as we rolled back to Alex's Place for the second time in three nights.

Dad having a beer is tantamount to the etiquette lady using foul language. It almost never happens. The last time Dad had a beer? Two years ago. It's not his thing. By and large he's a teetotaler.

Our server, Shelly O'Donald, took our order for food and a round of beers.

"Would you ask the chef to English Cut my prime rib?" Dad asked Shelly cheerfully.

Shelly looked a bit puzzled about the request. She had never heard of English Cut. "I'll ask," she said before taking the rest of our orders and heading off toward the kitchen.

Shelly returned a few minutes later with the tallest beer mugs I've ever seen and a large plate of tasty clams casino. We dove right in. As I was inhaling my fourth clam, Shelly returned with news for Dad. "I'm not sure the chef knows what English Cut is. Can you explain it?" she asked.

"It's just very thinly sliced," Dad answered politely.

Shelly disappeared for a minute then returned wearing a smile. "The chef knows what you want now. He'll take care of it," she told Dad.

The English Cut request seemed to spark curiosity in the restaurant about who exactly was sitting at the table in the corner. I could see other servers looking our way, and a couple of heads popped out of the kitchen. They were probably trying to figure out why Senator John Glenn was here. It wouldn't be the first time Dad was mistaken for the retired Ohio senator and former astronaut.

"Who are you guys and why are you in Batavia?" Shelley asked curiously.

"We're the Walshes," I told her. "We're here fishing."

"Fishing where?"

"A couple of rivers near Lake Ontario."

"Are you from the area though?"

"No we're actually from four different states," I told her. "That's our Dad over there (Dad smiled and lifted his mug to say hello), and those are my brothers. Dad lives in Connecticut, my older brother, Chris, lives in Texas, and my younger brother, Mike, is from Georgia."

"Where do you live?" she asked.

"I live in Massachusetts," I answered.

"Do you have family here?"

"No, we don't know a soul in Batavia."

"So you came all the way to Western New York just to fish?" she wanted to know.

"Well there's more to it than just the fishing, but the fishing is very good too."

"Let me get the food. Tell me the rest of the story when you're done."

Shelly brought back Dad's English Cut prime rib, barbecue ribs for Mike and Chris, and spicy penne chicken with gorgonzola for me. The food was excellent and the beers refreshing. Dad finished only half of his brew, which Chris generously polished off before Mike or I could offer.

When the food was cleared, Shelly offered to take a picture of us. She saw my camera on the table and figured we were headed in that direction. Good anticipation and good photography on her part. She took some beauties. I know because I checked the playback screen on the camera to be sure.

When the bill came, Dad snatched it fast, recapturing whatever guards he surrendered earlier in the trip and restoring his status as chief of the tribe. As he did the math on the tip and signed the credit card slip, my brothers were slipping on their jackets.

Shelly came over to me and asked, "So what's the rest of the story behind the fishing?"

"Oh yeah. The fishing was really secondary. We don't get together all that often. It's just really hard to do it. We live in different states and my brothers and I all have demanding jobs and young families. The last time all three brothers and Dad were together was five years ago. Interestingly enough we went fishing. The difference this time was the urgency—ours and the urgency of the fish. Most of the fish we caught swam out of the lake and up the river to lay their eggs in the same exact place where they were born. The fish went back to their roots, and so did we. The fishing itself gave us the opportunity to reconnect as fathers, sons, brothers, and friends."

"Oh that is so nice," Shelly said putting her hand over her heart, totally understanding and appreciating the metaphor.

"See my dad over there?" I said while pointing to the man at the table with reading glasses on his nose and pen in hand. "He's seventy-three."

"He's in good health though isn't he?" Shelly interrupted.

"Yes, *but he's seventy-three!* Is he going to be alive in five years? What kind of condition will he be in? What will his mobility be like? We couldn't wait another five years to find out. Tears came to her eyes and her voice cracked.

"Do you guys miss each other?"

"Of course."

"Are you close?"

"A lot closer than we ever were before."

"Did you guys fight as kids?" she asked.

"Oh yeah, absolutely. We fought all the time. I mean we loved each other, but we were brothers. That's what brothers do. They fight, right?"

"Yes. I have two sons."

"Do they get along?"

"Not as well as I'd like them to," she shared through trembling lips and moist eyes.

"And that kills you as a mother doesn't it?"

She nodded.

"That's what we did to our mom," I told her gesturing over to my brothers who were fishing mints out of bowl near the front door. "She'd get so upset when we would fight."

"Oh, she's no longer alive?"

"No, she died when Chris and I were in our early twenties, and when Mike was fourteen."

"I think she'd really be happy to know how things turned out for you guys."

"Yeah me too."

"And your dad, is he still widowed?"

"No. He remarried four years later. That's an amazing story too. He met a wonderful Irish Catholic woman who was widowed right around the same time he was. Here's the thing. If you saw Mary, his wife, you'd think she was our mother. And my stepbrothers and sisters? They look like they could be blood too. Maybe it's an Irish thing and we all look alike. We're a real life Brady Bunch."

"Oh my God," she said wide eyed and covering her mouth. "I just knew there was something special about your family."

"Now what about you Shelly, how old are your sons?"

"They're in their early twenties."

"Are they married, or single?"

"They're single."

"You know, it's gonna be all right. They'll be just fine. They'll come together eventually. Time and age will make them wiser and gentler. Maybe some distance between them will help too."

"Oh no, I just hope they don't move as far away as you guys did from each other."

"No, no, no," I laughed. "They don't have to go that far. Once they're out of the house and have their own places, you'll see a big difference."

"You think so?"

"Absolutely. I'm sure of it. I know these things."

"Is there anything I can do to bring them together as friends even sooner?"

"You know what? Tell them to go fishing," I told her before saying goodnight.

TWENTY

We're Screwed

Author Kevin Walsh waiting impatiently for damaged tire to be fixed, Batavia, New York, November 2012

The screw that lodged itself in the center of my truck's front right tire the day before would prove to be one helluva pain in the ass the final morning of our trip, and the opportunity for another brotherly showdown.

After checking out of the hotel, I came out to my truck in the parking lot to find the tire noticeably lower. Facing a 400-mile high speed drive, we just had to get it fixed. My AAA membership wasn't much help. The switchboard operator said they'd change a flat tire, but not patch a leaky one. Great.

Batavia had plenty of corner gas stations and minimarts but few that offered repair services. The nearest service station I could find was almost twenty miles away. The leaky tire at this point was half flat, and I didn't want to risk a drive that long. I had a Fix-a-Flat kit in my glove box and considered giving the repair a shot. I had seen patch jobs done several times before at my local service station, so I had a good sense of what was involved. Chris had patched a few tires too and said it wasn't all that hard. But here's the deal, once you pull that sharp object out, you better get it right or you're going to be completely flat fast.

As Chris and I were talking it over in the parking lot of the hotel, Mike had a good idea.

"Why don't we just drive over to Walmart? They have an express lube and tire center."

Good call. Boom. Off we go to Walmart. I pull up to the service center and find out it's a forty-five-minute wait, even though there's just one car in front of us getting its tires changed. I went back to the debate with Chris about fixing it ourselves and getting on our way. It was the day before Thanksgiving and I wanted to get on the road before the holiday travel really picked up.

Chris insisted that if we do it, we'd have to take the tire off.

"No way," I told him, "you just turn the damaged tire out, get on the ground and just do it. That's how I've seen it done. It takes like thirty seconds."

"Yeah, but if you don't get it right, you have all the weight of the vehicle pressing down, which forces the air out of the tire even faster," Chris reasoned.

The debate went on for about ten minutes in the Walmart parking lot. Dad was getting antsy and nervously paced around the truck while chain smoking. Mike mentally checked out and surfed the Internet on his iPhone.

Chris and I went back and forth. It was just like the old days with neither willing to budge. We weren't just debating the process of how to repair the tire properly, but whether it was smart and/or safe to even try. We weren't pros and ultimately reason won out over stubbornness. We had a responsibility to ourselves and everyone else on the road. I gave in. I let the guys in the Walmart garage do it.

For my good discretion I was punished for what I saw unfold in the garage. They actually put the truck on the lift and were taking forever to do what I had seen done many times before in less than a minute. I was going stir crazy and complaining vociferously to Mike and Dad who eventually were so annoyed with me they took a brief walk around the store before coming back. Chris was laughing at me from the other side of the waiting room while reading a *Field and Stream* article about how to tan skinned animals inside your home bathroom. Who the hell does that?

I hate being stuck and I hate to wait. We were both. But as bad as I felt by the interminable delay, I found some humor in it. I had to. I was getting all screwed up in the head over a screw in my tire. As I watched the mechanic pull the offending piece of metal out of the tread pattern, I remembered a far worse travel story years ago that left me feeling tired and well ... screwed. Naturally, the Reillys were with me.

"Hey, Dad, remember that trip to North Carolina I took with the Reillys when I was fourteen?"

"Oh good Lord," Dad chuckled while shaking his head.

Chris and Mike just rolled their eyes knowing a crazy story was coming. My brothers loved when the Reilly brothers came over to our house in Meadowbrook for dinner, which was often. I spent so much time in my teen years with Will and Hugh playing and practicing golf. My time with them meant time away from my family. That too could be a reason why I don't have quite the connection with Chris and Mike that they share with each other. But that's on me. The Reilly legend and affection lives on in our family all these years later.

It was 1984. We were driving from our homes in suburban Philadelphia to North Carolina for a junior golf tournament. It was a twelve-hour drive, about 750 miles in all. Knowing that the world famous '78 Camaro would never make it that far, we upgraded and took the Reillys' silver 1979 Audi instead. Trouble was, nobody checked the oil before we left.

Even though Hugh was a year younger than Will, Hugh always drove. About an hour and a half into the trip, just across the state line of Delaware and Maryland, the Audi died. As smoke wafted out from under the hood, Hugh steered the coasting car off to the side of I-95 in Elkton, Maryland. We walked to a nearby gas station and called for help. Within minutes a tow truck operator arrived. The first thing he did was check the oil.

"You boys know there's no oil in this car?" he asked.

There are few ways better to destroy a car's engine than to drive it a long distance without enough oil. As part of our roadside relief, we had to pay the guy $50 before he hoisted the car, and another $50 once we arrived at his place of business. I had a few fifty-dollar traveler's checks with me, but he'd have none of that. He wanted cash. So Hugh reached into his pocket and pulled five tens off a roll.

Back in the early 1980s, Elkton, Maryland, could have passed as the backdrop for the *Dukes of Hazzard* TV show. Cecil County looked like the fictional Hazzard County in land and people. The difference was the people in Elkton weren't acting. They were real life *characters.* Most of the ones we saw resembled Crazy Cooter, the mechanic who took care of Bo and Luke Duke's General Lee.

The place where our car was towed was a junkyard/repair shop combination. As luck would have it, the owner looked like Uncle Jesse Duke—except dirtier. He told us, "Eye'm nawht interested in repairin' your car boys," in drawl that was more hillbilly than Southern.

We were really stuck and really hungry. There were two young men working in the garage who kept popping their heads into the office for a look at the decently dressed lads in Bermudas and polo shirts. We were just as curious about them as they were about us. They were wearing coveralls and were so blackened from head to toe with grease, we could hardly tell whether the garage hands were black or white. Based on the shapes of their heads and eyes, we guessed they were brothers, and likely the sons of the owner. Because they were wiry, they were probably teenagers, a little bit older than I, and a couple of years younger than Will and Hugh.

"The older one is that boy pictured on the wall," Will said with a look of astonishment on his face while pointing to a framed photo.

We couldn't wrap our heads around the fact that a boy so dirty could clean up so well and ah ... go to the prom. It just seemed impossible that you could get all that muck off. And then to put on a white tuxedo? Whoa! What's more, a junkyard office just seemed like an odd place to hang a prom picture. I would've expected a nudie calendar or a photo of an auto racing legend before that.

Reaching our parents was no easy deal either. We didn't have cell phones back then and long distance calling was expensive. The junkyard owner didn't want to pay for it.

"I'll call my parents, give them your phone number quickly, and have them call you back. That way they pay for it," Hugh suggested.

That would've worked great had someone been home at the time to answer, but they weren't. So it took a few additional phone calls to track down Mr. Reilly. As Hugh is dialing away, the owner is glaring at him and Will and me for running up his bill. Hugh shrugs as if to say, "Yo, bud, what do you want me to do?"

Eventually we located Mr. Reilly who was in the middle of a spectacular round of golf. With nine holes to go, he had a shot at the course record. As competitive golfers ourselves, we knew that meant there was no way he was coming in early despite our predicament. Nine more holes and an hour-and-a-half drive meant we were at least four hours away from being rescued.

But wait there's more. Mr. Reilly would have to hook up with my dad, secure a trailer, and head south with a replacement car. So now we're about *six* hours out.

About two hours into this breakdown mess, the Reilly brothers and I still haven't sat down inside the messy office. It was just too filthy and we don't want to soil our clothes. There was a couch, but the cushions were sooty and greasy. We see why when the younger son came in from the garage. He plunked himself down to rest, not bothering to wipe his coveralls before taking a seat. It was grease on top of grease.

Hoping to get out of there and to get something to eat, I asked, "Hey, is there a McDonald's around here?"

"No," the owner said slowly, as if he'd never heard of the most popular restaurant in the world.

"How about a sandwich shop? Or any other fast food place?"

"No, we don't have any of those."

"Is there *any* restaurant around here? Is there even a downtown?" I asked, almost pleadingly.

Suddenly a twangy, high-pitched voice pierced the air. "There is a spaghetti house up the street!" the young son offered excitedly. "But," he sighed, "it's closed on Sunday."

Just our luck, it was Sunday afternoon. About a half hour later, sensing our frustration and wanting to close shop for the day, the owner said, "If you boys want, I can drop you off at the 76 truck stop on 95. They have nice juicy hamburgers there. It might be more comfortable for you to wait there for your parents than it is here."

We didn't have to be asked twice. On the way out we cut through the garage where the sons had retreated before closing. They were showering in the open. A stream of soapy foam, tinted with speckles of black, flowed across the slightly pitched concrete floor to a drain cut in the middle.

"See y'all later," one yelled over the hiss and steam of the hot shower, while exacting a spirited wave.

The nude visual made us do a double take. The boys in the shower laughed as we couldn't believe our eyes. It had nothing to do with them being nekkid. It was more about the transition to being clean. From sooty black to washed white. It was as if they bathed in auto lubricants all day, then washed off a layer at night.

After we were dropped off at the 76 truck stop, we immediately went to the bathroom to wash our hands. Wait, wash doesn't even begin to describe it. We *scrubbed* our hands with the effort of a surfer who had just suffered a cut on a coral reef. You almost wanted to remove a dermis layer to know nothing was growing on you, or inside of you.

Once clean, we settled in at the food counter and ordered those juicy burgers the junkyard owner beamed about. Turns out the hamburgers were quite dry. But considering we had not had anything to eat or drink for almost ten hours, we inhaled what was before us. The crispy fries and fountain Cokes, which had the perfect balance of syrup and carbonation, more than made up for the bad burgers.

After the meal, Will and Hugh went to the arcade and pumped dozens of quarters into the video games. I took my shag bag to an open grass field next to the truck stop and hit some golf balls. At the very least we were going to miss a day of practice on the golf course. An open field not far away from the northern headwaters of the Chesapeake Bay was the next best thing. It was a good practice session, but when I went to pick up the balls I couldn't find half of them. The grass was soft and a little on the deep side. It swallowed up about forty of the balls that I had hit.

As the sun was setting on our travel day from hell, a large blue Ford 150 truck was pulling off the southbound lanes of 95 and into the truck stop. Being pulled behind the truck was a low-riding green trailer that normally transported equipment. Traveling right behind the truck and trailer was a big red Ford Bronco.

Mr. Reilly climbed out of the blue truck, followed by my dad in the Bronco. Both had looks on their faces that may as well have said, "What the hell happened?"

By then we were exhausted from the ordeal and didn't really want to talk about it. But we had to because we had to lead Mr. Reilly and my dad to the junkyard to pick up the Audi for transport back to Pennsylvania. When our parents saw the junkyard and its operator, they just "got it." They knew we'd had a very tough day.

After Mr. Reilly settled up with the owner, we collectively pushed the powerless Audi onto the trailer. My dad handed the keys to the Bronco over to Hugh and gave me some more money. Mr. Reilly did the same with his sons and instructed us to drive for just an hour or so and then find a hotel for the night. Naturally, we didn't listen.

We drove two hours to Washington and did some impromptu sightseeing around the Capital. We'd never been to the District and were shocked to find that the Washington, D.C., you see on TV on *NBC Nightly News* is not the Washington you see in person. It is home to some of the roughest neighborhoods known to America. We were as out of place in D.C. as we were in Elkton.

"Let's get out of here," I announced.

Hugh would have none of it. He was too entertained by the freak show unfolding on a corner outside of a biker bar. The rough riders on Harleys must have seen us as fresh meat—an easy carjack—before anyone knew what carjacking meant. Sensing that I might be right about bailing on the town, Will ordered his younger brother to drive away from the inner city.

Shortly after midnight, we decided to turn in for the night. We stopped at the first hotel we saw, which was on a hill overlooking Capitol Hill. Trouble was, the hotel wouldn't have us. We were too young. It wouldn't rent out hotel rooms to anyone under twenty-five. We asked the man at the front desk if there were other hotels he could recommend instead. He said they all had similar age policies. So in essence, we were "screwed." Too exhausted to drive anymore, we decided to sleep in the parking lot.

There were two rows of seats in the Bronco. One in the middle, the other in the back. I took the back seat and Hugh took the middle one. Will took a couple of towels off his golf bag to use as pillows and opted to sleep outside of the car on the grass. Sometime in the middle of the night the rain came. Will awoke from his slumber and started banging on the car windows. Hugh woke up first, and then I did. We thought we were being robbed.

"Get the hell out of here!" Hugh screamed at the would-be attacker of the car.

Boom, boom, boom went the sound of a pounding fist on the driver side window.

"Let me in!" a young man demanded with an angry look on his face.

Hugh pounded back from the other side of the glass with aggression, unleashing a torrent of profanity, instructing him to back off.

It was then that we came to our senses and realized the alleged attacker was one of us.

"Hugh! It's me, Will! Open the door and let me in. It's pouring rain!"

Relief swept over us as we let Will in, just before he was swept away by the brief squall. Will was soaked and spent. So were we. Almost as soon as we let Will into the car, the rain stopped. It was too late for him, but within minutes the not-so-good view was very good. Hugh decided the view from the hill warranted another look down below. It was about 3 a.m. and we figured why not?

Hugh was driving; we'd either enjoy the sojourn or doze off while Hugh drove around. What did it matter?

I had one eye open and one eye closed in the backseat. Up front Will and Hugh started arguing. It got very loud with personal insults volleyed back and forth. Exasperated, wet, frustrated, and tired, Will unloaded on Hugh from the passenger seat with a sidearm slug to Hugh's right shoulder.

Now I had been witness to many a brotherly verbal tilt between the two, and the putter chucking incident, but other than that, I'd never seen either one lay a hand on each other. Stunned and sore, Hugh put the car in park, turned the engine off, pulled the keys out of the ignition and took off on foot. Talk about a kick in the golf balls. Will and I were stuck right in front of Capitol Hill, at a major intersection, about a three wood away from the Rotunda.

"Where's he going, Will?"

"I dunno," Will answered.

"When is he coming back?"

"I dunno."

"Do you have your own keys so we can at least pull over to the side of the road?"

"Nope."

"Holy crap!" I said loudly. "Will, we're going to get arrested. The Secret Service or Capitol Police will be here any minute."

But the authorities never came by, despite the fact we were parked—*parked* at traffic light, drawing the attention of honkers and hookers who wanted to know what the hell we were doing.

About an hour later we saw a silhouette approaching the Bronco. I ducked my head under a towel thinking a tire iron was about to come smashing through the window. Instead I heard the familiar sound of a key entering a lock, a door opening, and the familiar voice of Hugh saying, "Let's get the hell out of here."

With that, we drove all the way through to the Sandhills of Central North Carolina with Hugh behind the wheel. Nobody brought up the dustup in D.C. We had all moved on as the car moved south on 95.

I actually won that golf tournament at Whispering Pines. It was my first win on a national stage. But who remembers that other than me? All these years later when I say, "Elkton, Maryland," to Will he cringes and ducks. Hugh laughs and says, "Oh my God," before launching into a play-by-play of the trip that gets better each time he tells the story. Dad? I think he's trying to forget. But how can you? That trip was so bad it was good. My brothers? They always appreciate an entertaining story, especially if the Reillys were involved.

The cost of the tire repair at the Walmart? $10.80. The cost in lost time? An hour plus. But at least we had the peace of mind that professionals had done the job and we would not have to worry about a tire blowout on the Interstate.

It's true, that screw turned out to be a colossal pain in the ass. But the truth is, that's what made the mess memorable. The same is true of my time with Will and Hugh Reilly. I'd give anything to relive those days. Those patched together memories, and the patch on my tire made for a smooth ride and a warm chuckle as I merged onto I-90 East headed home.

TWENTY ONE

The Healing Ride Home

I'm a little disappointed with myself right about now. We're three quarters of the way through the trip, and I haven't spoken directly to my siblings about my not having been a good brother. Does it really have to be voiced? Or is my internal admission and self-loathing enough? I just don't know. I have about 350 miles of driving to decide.

The long ride home featured a decent volume of traffic, but few slowdowns. To pass the time, Chris brought up the story of his passing gas and followed it up with the YouTube fart video that he showed Norm and me before the sun came up on the second day of fishing.

To bring Dad into the loop, Chris showed him the Breaking the Barrier video. Dad found it exceptionally hilarious and almost hyperventilated when he saw it. What's exceptional about that is how counter it was to the gas passing culture we were raised in. Not only did Dad discourage farting, he forbade us to use the word *fart.*

"That's bathroom talk!" he would bark.

"Well that's what everyone else calls it," I protested.

"I don't care. I don't want that language in my house," he insisted.

"Okay, so what are we to call it then?"

"Call it a *tut-uh-tut.* That's what it sounds like."

I'm not kidding. We called farts *tut-uh-tuts* in my house. It was a draconian attempt at decency and our father's way to keep marginally crude language out of the act. But Dad's reaction to the video gave us an honest whiff of his true feelings about farts. He finds them just as funny as we do, and the rest of the millions of people who watched the Breaking the Barrier video after it went viral.

Exhausted from his laughing fit, Dad fell asleep. With Dad crashed, we listened to the National Public Radio's podcast report on Penn State being the number one party school in America.

There was no mention of the Jerry Sandusky scandal for the simple fact that the report was recorded before any of that became public.

The narrator took us on an audio tour of State College, Pennsylvania, on a typical Saturday night. The report highlighted the impact of heavy drinking with testimony from students, faculty, and town residents. The slurred speech of "man on the street" student interviews and "natural sounds" of metal trash cans being knocked over and lids being kicked down the street by laughing drunks made it feel as if we were there.

Frustrated townspeople spoke of all but having to guard their property from students urinating, fornicating, vomiting, and essentially running roughshod through their neighborhoods late at night. The podcast clearly illustrated the town-versus-gown dynamic that was Penn State, but really, it could have been anywhere. Considering who was listening in my truck, we vicariously substituted our own universities in place. This could just as easily have been Purdue, Villanova, or Boston College.

As we drove through Scottsville on 90 East, I spotted the Genesee River. It reminded me of where Paul Jacob learned to fish as a boy with his disabled neighbor. It also brought back memories of my childhood, in a most different context. When I saw the word *Genesee*, I immediately thought of Genesee Beer and the Philadelphia Eagles.

Back in the early 1980s, I went to a lot of Eagles games with our good family friends, the Van Burens. We sat up in the infamous 700 level of the old Veterans Stadium. Genesee Beer was served liberally and all those libations made for outrageous behavior. I saw so many fights and crazy things that I could probably write a book about that too. The Genesee moment at the concession stand really stands out.

I was ten years old and had gone to get something to drink by myself. There was a guy in front of me who was clearly in the bag and wanted a few more beers.

"Yo, how are ya? I need three Jennies," he told the server loudly.

"Sorry, hon, but we're awlh out-uh Jenny," the lady with big hair and heavy makeup said from behind the taps. "We ran out last quarter. Youse guys drank it awlh."

"Youse don't have any Jenny left?" he said with a tone that bordered on the tragic.

"Nah, hon, it's awlh gwhone."

He put his hands on his head, turned around with eyes wide and a look on his face as if he had just found out his dog had been hit by a car. He was crushed and cried out in agony as he walked away.

"Oh my God! I can't believe dehr awlh outta Jenny!"

So now it was my turn to order. "What can I git fer ya hon?" the woman asked me.

"Well, I guess I'll just have a Coke," I said shrugging, not sure whether it was okay to laugh at the very adult thing I just saw.

The woman gave me a look that may as well have said, "That's what too much Jenny or any other beer will do to you." With a wink she handed over a pre-poured soda that was covered with saran wrap. The ice cubes were mostly melted and the Coke was watery. Nobody was buying Coke. Everybody was buying Jenny. That Coke must have sat on the counter for a couple of hours.

Years later when I was finally legal or pretty close to it, I just had to try a Jenny to see if it was all that it was cracked up to be. When I cracked open the can, I felt like I was ten years old and back at the Vet. I could smell the hotdogs, feel the crowd, and hear the drunk at the front of the beer line crying about no Jenny. I took a sip and gave the Jenny suds a chance to settle in. And you know what? I think I would have preferred another watery soda instead.

Fifty-seven miles and an hour later we passed Seneca Falls in the Finger Lakes region. My inner sports dork immediately thought of Seneca Wallace, the onetime Iowa State star quarterback who later played nine not-as-thrilling seasons in the NFL with the Seattle Seahawks and the Cleveland Browns. I always thought he would have been a better pro than he turned out to be.

The student in me remembered Seneca Falls as the birthplace of the women's suffrage movement. Elizabeth Cady Stanton and Lucretia Mott led the way with the Declaration of Sentiments at the first Women's Rights Convention in 1848. They didn't live to see the nineteenth amendment, but because of them my daughters will be voting for the first time within a year of the hundred-year anniversary of women getting the right to vote.

More than anything, my love of the land aligns with the spirit of Native American Indian Tribes, which have such a rich history around the Finger Lakes region. This is Iroquois land, with Seneca and Cayuga tribes settled around Seneca and Cayuga Lakes. Chris and I were Indian Guides at the local YMCA. Dad was the Sasquatch Tribe leader. We studied Indian culture, made buckskin vests and tomahawks, wore headbands with feathers in them, shaped walking coup sticks, and honored the original people who lived on our land before our ancestors did.

Dad's Indian name was Thunder Cloud, which made sense because he could roar. I was Blue Cloud, which made no sense because if a cloud was really blue, you wouldn't be able to see it against the blue sky. And Chris was Fast Arrow, which was wishful thinking, because, as I told you earlier, Chris is actually quite slow of foot. Mike never got involved in Indian Guides.

Much of the water where we fish and the land we played on as children was originally Indian tribal land. We know this because of the names. So much of my outdoors experience was learned in those Indian Guides workshops. But more than anything, Indian

Guides was about bonding with your dad and the land. We're still doing that thirty-five years later.

Forty-seven miles and fifty minutes later we drove past Syracuse. I instantly thought of the Orange and Syracuse University. I've worked with no fewer than ten Syracuse University graduates over the years. The Newhouse School of Journalism pumps out a lot of fine broadcasters. It's a pleasure to have them alongside in the workplace, but it's impossible to watch Syracuse basketball games with them. They're insufferable.

My lasting memory of Syracuse is Indiana's Keith Smart burying a last-second jumper to beat them in the 1987 national championship game. As mayhem unfolded on the floor, 'Cuse's Howard Triche reclined on his back on the floor next to the Syracuse bench, propped up by his elbows. Triche was a good player, but I found his floor "pose" horribly disrespectful.

Fast forward to March 2012. I was sitting courtside, covering the NCAA Elite Eight at Boston's TD Garden. Syracuse was playing Ohio State for a chance to advance to the Final Four. Brandon Triche was playing for the Orange. Man did he look familiar. He's Howard Triche's nephew. Ohio State won the game 77–70.

That was an interesting game for reasons other than the Triche lookalike. Jim Boeheim subbed out senior point guard Scoop Jardine with little more than four minutes to go with the Orange trailing the Buckeyes by five. The ball handling suffered with Kris Joseph promptly turning the ball over twice in twenty-three seconds.

After the game a student reporter with *The Daily Orange* pressed Boeheim about taking out his starting point guard at such a critical time. Boeheim didn't like the question. The questioner didn't back down. As that was unfolding, Kris Joseph was next to coach with his face buried in a towel. Scoop Jardine was next to him crying his eyes out. It was unbelievable theater—combative, emotional, awkward, raw, and very real. Quite simply, it was *awesome.*

Despite Kris Joseph's tough final minutes of his final college game, the hometown Boston Celtics liked what it saw from him and selected him three months later in the second round of the NBA draft. The Celtics also took Joseph's Syracuse teammate Fab Melo and Ohio State center Jared Sullinger in the first round. You just never know how things will play out.

One hundred ten miles, and an hour and forty-five minutes later, we arrived at Johnstown, New York, the halfway point home. I was still stewing about what to say to my brothers and when to say it. I just wished Mike or Chris would have somehow picked up on the feelings I was trying to project to save me the agony. Then someone said it was time for a bathroom break and something to eat. So I pulled off the Interstate.

Historic Johnstown is named after Sir William Johnson. Johnson was famous for his relationships and trading with the Indians. He negotiated the Treaty of Fort Stanwix with six tribes in 1768, which limited British colony expansion. He also ended a Pontiac uprising and defeated the French at Lake George in 1755, furthering his legend and eventually leading to being named Superintendent of Indian Affairs for the Northern Colonies.

I'll remember Johnstown for something other than what I read on the blue historic plaque outside the rest stop. I'll remember the funny but miserable guy in the bathroom wearing an old Donovan McNabb Eagles jersey. He left a stall muttering with an accent as thick as Cheez Whiz. My best guess, there was no toilet paper inside. That'll give you a crappy disposition. And considering his Iggles were a dumpy 3–7 at the time, it was twice the pain.

In the spirit of brotherly love, I empathized with the man's agony. But considering where he just came from, I wasn't about to shake his hand. Philly people stand out wherever they are. It's more about the voice and the *attytude* than anything else. One time in the confessional at college the priest pegged me before I confessed a single transgression.

"Bless me Father for I have sinned ..."

"*Yo!* What part of Philly euwe from?" he interrupted.

"Is it that obvious?" I asked.

"Oowh yeah. I'd recognize the way euwe tawlk anywhere. We don't get a lot of Philly people out here in Indiana."

So we talked about our home neighborhoods and where we got our cheesesteaks. At some point I even confessed my sins. And when it was over, Father Phil gave me absolution. You heard right, a priest from Philly named Phil.

Father Phil couldn't see me, but he didn't have to. He *knew*. That's the thing about Philly people. We know our own. My brothers and I would have known the guy leaving the crapper in the bathroom was from Philly—Donovan McNabb jersey or not. We may not be able to explain why, but we know it when we see it, or hear it. One more thing, the Eagles fired Head Coach Andy Reid after the Birds finished the season 4 and 12.

The fun in Johnstown sparked a spirited conversation once we got back into the truck about sports in general, and the costs of attending major sporting events in particular. We all agreed it's too damn expensive. When we were kids, Dad could take us to Phillies games for a little bit more than the price of going to the movies. Those days are never coming back. The average cost of taking a family of four to a Major League baseball game is just over $200. That's too steep and has robbed fathers and sons and families in general from going to the ballpark semi-regularly. How sad.

The landscape of the sports we play and watch has changed in other ways too. When was the last time you drove down the street and had to wait for the kids to scatter from a street game of kickball? Has your car dodged a loose ball from a front lawn game in the last fifteen years? Gone are the days when everyone played some sort of pickup ball all around the neighborhood.

Much of that "free time" that we had as kids has gone to the scheduled activities with costly travel involved. In fact during the drive out to the fishing grounds on Sunday, Chris was following the play of his eight-year-old son, Christopher, at a junior golf tournament in Houston. The rest of the family was there too. Fourteen-year-old Caitlyn Walsh was texting her father little Christopher's hole-by-hole scores. The little man finished with a 101, twenty-three shots behind another little stud who shot 78. Whew!

Fifteen minutes and thirteen miles later I saw a sign for Amsterdam. Naturally I thought about Holland, windmills, wooden clogs, and tasty imported beer. I sang the Amstel Light jingle in my head, "95 calories never tasted so imported, till they imported Amstel Light." Amstel's okay, but I'd rather have a Heineken.

We passed Schenectady before reaching Albany. I don't think of Albany as the state capital. For me it's the former home of the Albany River Rats, the American Hockey League affiliate of the NHL's Carolina Hurricanes. How can a river rat have any possible redeeming value? It passes the stickiness test, that's for sure. But alas, the River Rats franchise couldn't stick in Albany. It's now the Charlotte Checkers. That's not sexy.

Thirty miles past Albany we drove by Chatham. Chatham, New York, is two hundred twenty-six miles and three hours and forty-five minutes away from Chatham, Massachusetts. The sight of the Chatham town sign made me think of one thing—sharks. There are no sharks in Chatham, New York; but if you watched the summer 2012 reports on the Boston news channels, Chatham, Mass., may as well have been the new fictional Amity, New York, of Jaws fame.

My goodness, if I never see another story about a Great White Shark sighting off the coast of Cape Cod I'll be really happy. Although, I was mildly freaked out to see a picture of a huge dorsal fin following a kayaker in the exact spot where I surfed the day before just around the Cape's elbow in Orleans. Turns out that was a Basking Shark, not a Great White after all. Either way, it was still a big-ass shark.

Crossing the Massachusetts state line in the town of Richmond reminded me of Richmond, Virginia—home of the Spiders and the University of Richmond. I have plenty of friends who went to college there. Chris does too. Mitch Richmond, the 1989 NBA Rookie of the Year and six-time All Star came to mind. So did Richmond, Indiana, which is the first town you pass on I-70 West when crossing the Ohio/Indiana state line. When I reached that Richmond in my college years, I knew I was in the home stretch of my long drive from the East Coast to West Lafayette, Indiana, home of Purdue University.

We drove through the Berkshires. I almost wanted to stop and pick up a couple of BerkShares, a local currency launched in 2006 to spark the economy of the Berkshire region. *The New York Times* called BerkShares "a great economic experiment."

I saw a sign for Holyoke and I remembered being told a few years back by a fellow broadcaster to say it right. It's HOY-yohk or HOHL-yohk, but most certainly not hohl-EE-ohk. Then came Chicopee, about seven miles south of Holyoke. It's a tricky pronunciation too. Say it CHICK-uh-pee, not chi-KOH-pee, and be sure to get off 90 East for 91 South. I did. We were getting closer to home, about eighty miles and an hour and twenty minutes to go.

Springfield welcomed us with a vibe that's hardly as cheery as its name. "It looks like a factory town with no factory to work in," Mike said.

Situated on the banks of the Connecticut River, Springfield is the largest city in western Massachusetts. It's not without its problems. Of the 153,000 people who live there, more than a quarter of them live below the poverty line. Its nickname is The City of Firsts. It's probably best known as the place where basketball was invented and the home of the Basketball Hall of Fame.

Dad noticed the Hall as we drove by.

"Hey let's go check out the history of women's college basketball," he announced.

"Hey, let's not," I answered sarcastically.

Dad was being a dork. He was trying to get a rise out of his sons. Our father is a diehard University of Connecticut women's basketball fan. Most men in their seventies in Connecticut are too. Dad thinks Huskies' Coach Geno Auriemma is a hoops god, and the women who play for him are hot. I told him if he really wanted to see good college basketball in Connecticut, he ought to watch the men.

Chris found the whole old man/young women basketball watching thing a bit creepy. Dad would have none of it. Eventually we'd had enough of him and the debate about which is better—men's or women's basketball. Chris slinked back into his seat, pursed his lips, and shook his head.

"Man, that's five minutes I can't get back," he said before dropping a glob of tobacco spit into the bottom of his spittoon.

Before Chris spat again we were within spitting distance of the Connecticut state line. Longmeadow, Mass., leads to Enfield, Conn., and before we knew it, we were approaching Hartford. Just north of the city we met our first real traffic of the day on what's traditionally the busiest travel day of the year, the day before Thanksgiving. It was around three in the afternoon and plenty of people had left work early. We were stuck on 91 just north of the capital. The downtime was filled with ridiculousness.

"Yo, Kev, what was that *stupid language* you used to use with Michael when we were younger?" Chris asked.

Oh boy, here we go, I thought. This might be the confrontation that leads to confession. I was nervous as hell. Asking a question is a clever way of engaging an unwilling participant in conversation. It demands a response.

"I don't know," I answered, hoping it would all go away. Not a chance.

"Yeah, Pockycano. You used to say that all the time," Chris taunted. "That was so weird. What the hell is Pockycano? What does that even *mean?*"

The pressure was mounting.

"Oh wait, wait, I got some more," Mike piled on while sporting a humorously maniacal look on his face. "Eshani, pookunaka, shang face. You used to call me shang face. What's a shang face?"

"I don't know, I don't know," I answered while laughing nervously.

What can you say when someone calls you out on something that you know was weird, a time in your life that you're not exactly proud of? I was stuck. They let me have it good. But here's the beauty of having your balls busted. It shows you're *one of the guys.* This is how men show affection and acceptance. They wouldn't have done it if I wasn't their friend.

The laughter in the lashing was the difference that gave my heart the lift it needed. My brothers totally let me off the hook that I had been stuck on for pretty much my whole life. They kinda sorta did that earlier with the looks we exchanged in the cab of my truck when Mike drove back to the hotel after that first day of fishing. But this moment on the trip home, *this* was the real validation. This was my takeaway from the trip. And with that, I didn't even give damn about the traffic we were stuck in. I was home free.

As childish as my language was years ago, Chris's behavior in the back seat was juvenile too. Through the rearview mirror I saw him stick a plastic straw in Mike's ear while Mike was looking in the other direction. Mike's recoil and shock from the auditory invader produced an unrepeatable word.

"Cruiser bruiser!" Chris announced before slugging Michael in the arm.

"Ow! What the hell?" Mike protested.

"Oh, it's the newest version of slug bug or pidoodle," Chris said.

Mike didn't care what it was, and he didn't appreciate being punched by his older brother. He punched back even though there wasn't another PT Cruiser or a VW Bug in sight.

Now we're talking! A little backseat fight. This was old school. If Dad wasn't asleep, his arm probably would have been reaching back to break it up. Oh, the memories! That's really what the long ride to and from the fishing grounds was all about—the memories, the laughter, the conversations, and the clashes that we brothers had when we were children, and now as men.

Rides like these reminded us of who we are, where we came from, and what we went through over the years. Even though we now live far apart with families of our own, for a couple of days it was the original gang together again.

It took about twenty minutes for the traffic jam to break up and for us to get around the city. Once we got on Highway 2 East, it was a straight shot home to Ledyard.

I called Jean. She, Amanda and Samantha, and the dog were on the way from our home in Wellesley, Mass., to Ledyard. They were stuck in traffic where the Mass Pike meets 395 South. Mike called his wife, Rachel. She was coming from her friend's house in Sturbridge, Mass., with the kids. They were backed up in roughly the same place that Jean was too.

The final legs of the journey with my dad and brothers took us through Marlborough, Norwich, and Montville. As we crossed over the Thames River by Mohegan Sun Casino, I recalled what Dad said when we crossed the Mohegan-Pequot Bridge in the opposite direction three days before: "The fishing will be a lot better where we're going."

Boy was he ever right about that, and my goodness were we ever thankful that Dad had the foresight to see the potential of a trip this special unfolding before it actually did. It was almost as perfect as his perfect catch.

By late afternoon, we rolled into Dad's driveway in Ledyard, about ten hours after leaving Western New York. Jean, Rachel, and the collective kids followed about an hour later. It was the completion of a most perfect trip. We were safe, we were happy, and we were back where the journey started—home. As friends and family.

TWENTY TWO

Thanksgiving

I woke up Thanksgiving morning with the help of a wet kiss. It wasn't my wife, Jean; it was my German Shepherd, Beverly. It took a couple of licks, but eventually I leaped to my feet to take Beverly outside to go potty. It was still dark at 6 a.m., but 6 a.m. felt a lot better than a couple of days of waking up at 3:45. I tiptoed down the steps, careful not to wake the sleeping children.

My stealth was blown when Annie the Corgi erupted once I walked into the kitchen. She was not to be denied. I let her out of the kennel and took her outside with Beverly. As the dogs were sniffing around and marking territory on the front lawn, the shine of headlights came from around the corner. A car pulled into the driveway with the orange glow of a lit cigarette sticking out of the lips of my Dad.

Dad got out of the car, flicked some ashes on the ground, and reached down to brace himself for the oncoming charge of happy dogs. He was returning from the airport in Hartford where he had dropped off Chris for a 5:30 a.m. flight back to Texas.

"What's up, Dad? You tired?" I asked.

"Not really, are you?"

"I'm a little tired, but you know I feel like I slept in. Beverly woke me up at six. How did it go with Chris?"

"It was good. I think he was glad to be going home to be with his family."

"Are you sad that he couldn't stay for Thanksgiving dinner?" I asked.

"Well it would have been nice, but he has a family that needs him too," Dad answered with a shrug.

"It was still pretty nice to have your sons together again for a couple of days without much interference though, wasn't it?"

"It sure was. It sure was," he said before slipping back into the house to make coffee.

When the dogs were done with their business, I brought them back inside. Mary was making breakfast, and Dad was sitting at the table with a coffee mug in hand. It was a quiet, peaceful morning that would stay that way for a couple of hours. I uploaded the fishing pictures from my iPhone and camera into the computer to make for a bigger screen that I could show Mary.

"Wow!" she said when I showed her that final fish Dad caught with Paul.

Dad just grinned and shook his head as he pushed his whites through the egg yolk on his breakfast plate. Mary's not much into the fishing culture, but even she could see that fish was a beauty.

"Kevin, did you catch any fish as nice at that?" she asked.

"No," I answered with a laugh. "I caught some good ones, but nothing quite like that. Dad was the king fish of the trip and caught a fish worthy of a king," I said while gesturing toward my dad. "Now don't go getting a big head, Dad."

The praise put Dad back onto his pedestal, which is entirely appropriate considering we were back at his house. The dig made him guffaw and almost cough up his coffee. It was funny and it was clear he was still thrilled from the trip. He was thankful for the good time he had with his sons, and for good fishing.

By the time nine rolled around, the house was coming alive with little people and dogs stirring. The gentle sound of footy pajama feet tapping on the steps and rounding the corner toward the kitchen sent the dogs in the direction of the new breakfast arrivals. Mary swapped out the cooked food for the miniature cereal boxes, and the dogs parked themselves below the children hoping for falling food. There was cheer in the air and Cheerios on the ground. It was wonderful morning to wake up to.

The star of the morning was the youngest member of the extended family. Little Peter came into the kitchen and met his Massachusetts family (Samantha, Amanda, Jean, and me) for the first time. Dressed in a red onesie, he was fussed over by my daughters and everyone else. He had a look of wonder on his face. So did Victor, the exchange student from China. I'm sure Victor had never seen such family commotion. It was his first Thanksgiving and we were just getting started on the day.

The weather on Thanksgiving was an added bonus. The temperature was in the low 40s and was expected to reach into the mid-50s by late morning. It was a good day to get outside to burn off some energy and to let Mary get an uninterrupted early start on preparing Thanksgiving dinner. There was a high school football game between Ledyard High and Fitch, the public high school in nearby Groton. Mike suggested we go to the game. We took two cars, four small children, and Victor. I hadn't been to a high school football game in almost twenty years.

The pageantry and the passion were everything I remembered about high school football. The cheerleaders were pretty and chipper. My girls, Samantha and Amanda, watched the older girls closely, caring little about the football action on the field and more about the cheering on the sideline. What really stood out to me though was the speed of the athletes. Covering pro sports as I do comes with a caveat. Once you get accustomed to the precision of the NFL, and the blazing speed of its players, everything else looks impossibly slow. Still, I liked the high school game. It made me feel young again.

I was also trying to help Victor understand a game that was foreign to him. He understood tackling and why it was done, but I'm not sure I did a good enough job explaining the concept of four downs and why it was wise to punt on fourth and long. He knew enough to guess that with Ledyard trailing by 13 at the end of the third quarter, a comeback was unlikely and that it might be smart for us to leave early to get a jump on traffic. We should have stayed. Ledyard scored 14 fourth quarter points and won the game. Something else to celebrate over dinner.

As we sat down for dinner late in the afternoon, I did so at peace. I felt much better about my relationship with my brothers, the effort to make Dad proud of us, and what we did to let him know how proud we are of him. And as far as having good clean fun? That goes without saying. The goals I set for the trip were by and large accomplished; we left as family, bonded as men, and returned as friends. That was worth a toast, which we did, *with wine.* Hey, there were women around, we had to class it up.

"To a great trip and family," I announced while raising a glass of red.

Then when it was time to say grace, Dad crinkled his face, tapped his water goblet, and looked over at me from the opposite end of the table.

"Kevin, would you say grace please?"

"Sure," I answered, accepting the grace-saying duties as another passed baton.

Jean and I usually say a Catholic version in our house with the children, but on this day I chose the simple nondenominational blessing that my brothers and I grew up with as kids:

Thank you for the world so sweet,
Thank you for the food we eat
Thank you for the birds that sing,
Thank you God for everything. Amen, let's eat.

"Oh, I like that one," Dad said smiling. "I haven't heard that one in so long and had forgotten how it went."

"That's why I said it."

I like the prayerful poem because it's profound. It says so much in so little. I suppose that's why I remember it perfectly despite not saying it since I was a boy. I can only hope that the bonds and memories of the fishing trip with my Dad and brothers will stick with us for as long as the words of the simple dinner prayer have stuck with me. That would be sweet, and for that we'd all be thankful.

TWENTY THREE

Return to the Trout Pond and Promises of a Better Brotherhood

Author Kevin Walsh with New England Cable News Anchor Kristy Lee, Newton, Mass., December 2012

It would be a couple more hours before the New England Patriot players woke up on the first Monday of December. There was no practice scheduled, but many would head in to Gillette Stadium in Foxborough, Mass., to watch film and to get treatment. The Patriots beat the Miami Dolphins 23–16 the day before in South Florida, clinching their fourth straight AFC East Division title and ninth in ten years.

These are good times, but Mondays are bad for the body. Ask any player and he'll tell you--when you wake up on a Monday, everything hurts. Of course winning makes it easier to get out of bed, even if it's done painstakingly slow.

Mondays during the NFL season are tough on me and my family too. The first of two alarm clocks went off at 3 a.m. I have to get up and get into work by four, so I can be on TV giving New England Cable News viewers the highlights from each Sunday's Patriots game. I always set two alarms in the event I might accidently reach over and turn the alarm off before my feet hit the floor. The second alarm was set for 3:15. The redundancy reduces the chance of oversleeping, although I have overslept a couple of times. It would have been many more times had Jean not saved me.

It took me a couple of minutes to get going that December day. Sometimes Jean gets up with me to make it easier. Without coffee, I could never do this. This Monday was different though. The weather was unseasonably warm, and considering I was at the end of my work week, I had some late morning and afternoon fun in mind. As my second cup of coffee warmed up in the microwave oven, I loaded my golf clubs, fly rod, and gym bag into the covered bed of my truck. With the truck loaded and ready, I came back inside the house to shower, shave, dress, and eat quickly. Breakfast was Honey Nut Cheerios, sliced bananas, and coffee.

I was excited about the day because a Patriots win just makes everyone around these parts feel better. I climbed into my truck and turned on the radio. I always listen to sports talk on the way into work to see if there's anything I missed in my preparation. As I drove to the NECN studios in Newton, I was thinking about the key plays of the Patriots/Dolphins game. It was my prep time before air time. You can't just come into work and figure it out once you get there. You have to come in with a plan and be ready to go.

Fifteen minutes after leaving my house in Wellesley, I pulled into the parking lot of NECN. The staff at the TV station was excited to see me. Production assistants and producers enjoy that I always bring good cheer and inject energy into their show. They're also eager to see if my take on the game matches theirs. Not always, but that's part of the fun—the debate. After a couple of touches of MAC makeup on my face to take the shine off, I was on the air and inside the homes of viewers across six states.

I love doing sports on TV. It's the perfect balance of fun, pressure, and meaningful work. I get to let my inner performer out, sharing video and information that viewers really want while showing off appropriately. Sometimes it works. When it doesn't, I fail spectacularly. Viewers like the honesty and the vulnerability. It's who I am, and among friends I'm not afraid to make mistakes.

My paid work for the day was done at 9:30 that morning, but I was just getting started. I took off to the gym to work out. The drive to the Boston Sports Club in Wellesley takes me past the trout pond at the Needham Sportsman's Club. As I drove by, I saw a pickup truck parked next to the clubhouse. I pulled in. It was Dick. Dick's a fellow member, but he wasn't fishing on this day. He was letting his little dog Marlie take a run around the pond.

The sun was out and the temperature was already in the 50s. The air was clear and the pond was crystal. My plan was to return late in the day to fish the afternoon hatch. But now that I was here, I couldn't resist.

I took my suit coat off and grabbed the rod out of the back of the truck. As I headed toward the water's edge with my tie still on, I could very well have been the best dressed fisherman in the world. Marlie didn't care. She made a beeline for me and launched herself. She bounced off my legs leaving muddy paw prints on my charcoal suit pants. Dick was apologetic, but I thought it was funny. I was happy that Marlie was happy. And I was even happier to be fishing well ahead of schedule.

Turned out the fishing was not so good this morning. I didn't catch a thing. Still, I just love casting and immersing myself in the activity. I expected the afternoon would be better when it got buggier and the fish raced to fill up on insects before the cold and the winter freeze came. Those warm thoughts followed me to the gym where I'd be plenty warm after an hour and a half of exercise.

After the workout I went over to Wellesley Country Club and played eighteen holes. I'm not a member, I'm a caddy. Caddies and club employees get to play for free on Mondays. I actually had a pretty good round going before some sloppy swings and poor putting sunk what could have been a score around even par. No need to fret. I had fun, got some additional cardio in, and I had a pond filled with trout waiting for me.

About an hour before sunset I returned to the trout pond. As I got my fishing gear ready at the back of the truck, I saw Brad, a fellow member, stalking a fish on the other side of a rocky point extending out into the pond. He waved to me but was clearly locked in on his fishing. I grabbed my rod and headed in his direction, intent on fishing farther down on the right side of the water. I found a spot with about fifty feet of casting room. I fired my trusty green, red, and white wooly bugger to a spot just in front of a bush that extended ten feet out into the water. I heard the voice of Jim, the retired forester, in my head, "Fish are where there's structure and protection."

The first cast produced nothing. Neither did the second. But on the third cast the orange strike indicator announced a hit. I heard Norm Raffelson's voice, guiding me through the hook set. "Just a little flick of the wrist."

I lifted my wrist a smidge, the line went taut and I felt a pull. The rod flexed and started shaking. I hadn't been here for five minutes and I had a fish on! I landed a pretty ten-inch rainbow with rich purple stripes down each side. The fight lasted about a minute, and to be truthful it wasn't much of a fight at all. I plucked the fly out from under the fish's top lip and gently placed him back into the water. He swam away slowly and I was juiced.

After that catch I flashed back in my mind, remembering being in the river with my dad and brothers. That was tough fishing. I never assumed any fight in the river was over until the fish was in the net. I knew better. Quite a few big ones got away in New York.

Here at the pond it was a totally different mindset. I had no doubt that once I hooked a fish, I would land it. I guess what I'm saying is, it's a lot easier to fish in the pond than it was to fish in the river. That doesn't make it any less pleasurable and satisfying. I know the joy of catching a big one in the river and a little fella in the pond. And you know what? I was just as thrilled to hold that ten-inch rainbow in one hand as I was holding a ten-pound steelhead in two.

With a fish on the board I went in search of more. A couple of minutes later I caught another one under a tree near the back of the pond. It struck after a roll cast. Another rainbow, about the same size as the one by the bush, but not as much color. And just as it was nearly dark, I had a final strike near the front left corner of the pond as I was working my way back toward the clubhouse. It could very well have been the same fish I caught near that spot about a month ago on a similar day when the temperature defied the calendar. Either way I was so thankful for such a wonderful day and the bountiful catch.

High on life I retired to the clubhouse. I thought about the day I had and the trip I just took with my family. I called my dad in Connecticut and told him the good news about the three fish. He's always thrilled to hear about my fishing adventures, no matter how small they are. I thought about calling my brothers too. But I figured they'd be just as annoyed with me for catching fish on a school day as they were the last time I called them from the clubhouse a month and a half ago, so I took a pass.

The next day I came back to the club hoping for more good fishing. I didn't get a bite. I called Dad with the news about no good news to report, but he was thrilled about something else.

"Hey, I got something wonderful in the mail from you today," he shared.

It was a handwritten note that I had sent my dad a few days earlier, along with a framed picture of us at dinner that I also sent to each of my brothers. In the note I thanked Dad for making the trip possible by planning it, paying for it, and all but refusing to take no for answer. I wrote about how much fun the fishing was, and how special it was to be together as men, brothers, fathers, sons, and friends at long last.

"That's exactly what I was hoping to accomplish with the trip," Dad said.

"Hey, Dad, one more thing I need to ask."

"Yes?"

I thought I knew the answer already in my heart, but sometimes your ears need confirmation.

"Are you proud of your sons, and the men we have become?" I asked nervously.

"*Absolutely*," he answered with tone and pride as thick as the walls of my throat.

Dad's picture of us on the fishing trip sits in his basement in Connecticut, alongside framed pictures of the extended Walsh/McGrattan families and twenty grandchildren.

Chris's is on a coffee table in the family room of his home in Texas. Mike's framed photograph is propped up on the family piano in Georgia. Mine rests on the top shelf of a small bookcase next to the dinner table in Massachusetts. All the photos are placed in places of high visibility. That means a lot of looks at a special moment frozen in time. And each time we see it, we'll celebrate the warm bonds of peace, posterity, family, and friendship swimming through our hearts, much like the fish that swim through the river.

Something else might have been accomplished on that fishing trip too—a legacy that lives on long after Dad is gone. Our dad has outlived his brothers by almost a decade, and we hope he lives a long, long life. But we know the reality. He's had those couple of strokes, enjoys eating a little too much, loves to smoke, and hates to exercise. My brothers and I have been really lucky to have him this long. At some point we're going to have to say goodbye. When it's time, what becomes of us? Would we plan a similar trip on our own? And whose responsibility would that be to take the lead?

I've spent a lot of time talking with my brothers since we went fishing. That trip to New York reconnected us, gave us a common ground in our conversations, and produced a profound reset on how we feel about each other. We don't need a reason to reach out anymore. We can just do it. And if we want to reminisce, we have no shortage of fish tales to wade through.

I'm sure in time the stories we'll tell will get better, and the fish will grow bigger. If we're really lucky, maybe we'll travel the world together like Dad does with his regular fishing pals. If not to that level, we can always come back to the same spot on the river near Lake Ontario where our septuagenarian pals Jack and Bob have fished forever. The brotherly get-togethers don't have to be every year, but they shouldn't take another five years like the last time.

I put out feelers on the future with Mike during a phone call in February 2013. "Yeah, I would like that," Mike said. "It doesn't have to be fishing either. As long as we're together."

"Ah that's great. Okay. Love you, Mike."

"I love you too, Kev."

The next day I called Chris on my way home from playing pickup ice hockey at Babson College in Wellesley. "Yo, I talked with Mike last night. He and I want to make the effort to take trips with the brothers more often, and with Dad for as long as he's able. You know, kind of start a tradition. What do you say? You on board?"

"Yeah, I'd love to. You paying?" Chris asked with a laugh.

"You wish," I laughed back. "We'll see. I'm gonna call Dad and tell him the goods news. Gotta go. Love you."

"All right, love you too," Chris answered as I hung up with him.

I drove to the Wellesley Ace Hardware where I needed to buy some Teflon tape to repair a lamppost. After pulling into a parking space in front of the store, I tapped the touch screen of my phone to dial Dad.

"Hello, Kevin," Dad answered, knowing it was me because my name popped up on his cell phone caller ID.

"Hey, Dad, guess what?"

"What?"

"I just talked with Michael and Chris. We've decided we're going to try to get together more often for trips like the one we just did. Once a year, maybe every two years, something like that. We want to keep the legacy intact with you, and even after you're gone. What do you think?"

Hey nothing like bringing up someone's mortality.

"Wait, what?" he asked, wondering if he'd heard me correctly.

He did. I repeated myself. Once it soaked in and he had a chance to process it, he said, "I think that'd be a *great* idea."

That's Dad. A man of few words and rare emotion, but I know he was touched.

A couple of days after those conversations, my brother Chris had been thinking a lot about the fishing trip. He called me at home. My daughter Samantha answered the phone.

"Hey, Pockycano! What are you doing?" she asked her uncle.

"Oh God, you're not talking like your father now are you? Put your dad on please," Chris told his niece.

"I thought Mike was Pockycano. Me now too? What the hell are you doing over there?" Chris asked me.

"I was telling the girls about my goofy childhood language and they think it's awesome. Weird, but awesome," I told Chris.

"Shang face!" came a girl's interrupting voice preceded by the click of someone crashing our call.

"Sammy, hang up the phone!" I scolded, causing laughter to erupt on all ends.

"You know that's the second phone call bomb my girls have done with you and their Uncle Mike. Get this. On Sunday, on the way to church, Amanda called Mike four times in three minutes. Each time it went to voice mail, she left a 'Shang Face!' in his mailbox. He called back as we were walking into St. Paul's and said, 'Usually when I get that many calls from one of you guys in such a short time period I think Dad is dead. Fortunately I was talking to him on the other line so I knew he was alive.'"

Chris and I laughed at the dark humor, and then the conversation turned more serious. We also talked about how the fishing trip made us reflect on our own lives lived and our futures, with silent thoughts replaced by spoken ones.

"You know the whole time we were fishing I was thinking about Dad and our lives, and just how predictable things were growing up," Chris offered. "Dad went to work, Mom had dinner ready when he came home, we did things together, and we knew we'd all eventually go off to college and start families. Now as we're getting closer to the end with him, I think about the lives we're living, and whether we're living up to the standard he set for us. I think about those scenes in *Saving Private Ryan*, you know on the bridge and in the cemetery? Go back and look at those final scenes. Tell me that doesn't make you think about Dad."

I did what Chris said. I went back and watched those scenes multiple times. I was struck by how emotional they were. Private James Ryan, played by Matt Damon, saw Captain John H. Miller, played by Tom Hanks, as a father figure. As Captain Miller was dying on the bridge, he pulled Private Ryan close and whispered in his ear, "James, *earn this. Earn it.*"

I can see how that scene touches my brother deeply. As the oldest son he must honor the past—Dad—and lead the future—Mike and me. Chris wants to know if he, in particular, and the rest of us have done enough to thank our dad for being the man he is, and for helping us become the men that we are. Have we made Dad proud? Have we *earned it* in his eyes?

"We have," I assured Chris with confidence, because I already knew the answer.

I could hear my brother's relief in his labored sigh. Then he returned the favor to me. "You know as much as I was thinking about Dad during the trip, I was thinking about my relationship with you and Mike," I told Chris.

"You were? How so?" he asked.

I took a deep breath and spoke from the heart. I was surprised how easily the words came out. "You were a really good brother to me and Mike. I wasn't half the brother you were to me, or him. I'm not proud of that, but I'm really proud of you and Mike especially. Mike could have gone the other way and turned out to be a really bad kid after Mom died. But he didn't. He's been through so much. When I look at your relationship with him, I see that you guys are really tight. I'm not a part of that. It's like I'm a third wheel. I mean, I know I'm your brother and you guys love me, but am I your friend?" the words spilled out.

I went on: "I was thinking about it the whole time while we were fishing and driving, but I didn't know how to bring it up. I was afraid you guys would laugh at me. I was a real shit at times to you and Mike when we were kids."

"Well, you know we all had different agendas," Chris said, letting me down easy. "I was doing my thing, you were doing yours. With the golf it's like you had a different life. And with Mike, he had other things going on too. But it's not like there's leftover resentment anymore. There's no grudge."

"Well, you know you guys did me a tremendous favor and let me off the hook without even knowing you did it on the ride home."

"Whaddaya mean?"

"Remember when we got to the traffic backup in Hartford and you and Mike unloaded on me about the Pockycanos and Shang Faces?"

"Yeah ..." Chris answered, not sure where this was going.

"Well, I was thinking about bringing up the regrets I had about the brother I was, and whether we were 'all good' or not. Then you guys laid into me with the language thing. But here's the deal. You guys were laughing and smiling while you were busting my balls. That's when I knew we were really okay. It was a great relief. You wouldn't have done it if I wasn't one of the guys."

"You are one of the guys," Chris said, giving the spoken blessing to complement the nut crushing one.

That was one helluva conversation. And probably the best I've ever had with anybody. After saying goodbye, I watched *Saving*

Private Ryan again. I wondered if there was something in it for me, as much as there was for Chris.

Sure enough there was, the cemetery scene with a much older James Ryan kneeling down and speaking at Captain Miller's grave: "Every day I think about what you said to me that day on the bridge, I've tried to live my life the best I could. I hope that was enough. I hope that at least in your eyes I've *earned* what all of you have done for me."

That primed my ducts, and then when the camera pulled out, the tears rushed in. A humbled Private Ryan rose from his knees. His elderly wife approached him as his extended family of children and grandchildren looked on. He turned to her and said, "Tell me I have led a good life. Tell me that I'm a good man."

"You are," she said.

Isn't that what it's all about? I'm just so thankful the chance to "earn it" with friendship, love, and mutual admiration among fathers, brothers, and sons was spawned because a wise man had the foresight to plan a most meaningful fishing trip before it was too late. We were "on fish" that whole trip, but I think we're on to something bigger from here on out. And that may be the most perfect catch of all.

Thank You Note to Dad

Author Kevin Walsh working on *The Perfect Catch* with dog Beverly at his fishing club, Needham, Mass., November 2012

The Perfect Catch author Kevin Walsh writing with dog Beverly at his fishing club, Needham, Mass., November 2012

November 28, 2012

Dear Dad,

Thank you so much for taking me and the boys on a wonderful fishing trip. It was the trip of a lifetime, and it came at a time when we all needed something like this to happen. I'm not sure which was better, the fishing or the time we spent together as a family.

Actually that's pretty easy—it was the latter, which is really saying something because the fishing was excellent. I'm sure we'll remember the long ride across New York and the time we spent over dinner as much as the fish we caught. Speaking of that—your last catch was absolutely the perfect way to end a perfect trip. You deserved to catch that fish.

Your foresight to plan the trip, paying for it in advance, and insisting that we come ensured that it happened. You're a great father who raised us right. I am proud to be your son.

Love,
Kevin

ACKNOWLEDGMENTS

Before anyone and anything, I'd like to thank my father, Bob Walsh, for being a great dad and introducing my brothers and me to fishing. It really is the gift that keeps on giving. We've enjoyed the sport with each other, alone, and now with our own children.

To Chris and Michael Walsh. By simply being themselves they were good brothers, good company, and good consciences when I sometimes went off the rails with crazy writing and not always the best of behavior. I wish for many more times of fishing and time among brothers in the years ahead.

To my wife, Jean, and beautiful daughters, Samantha and Amanda. For giving me joy, love, and support in my life. This book may have been about fishing with fathers, sons, and brothers; here's to more fishing with fathers, daughters, sisters, and wives. I got a feeling I'm going to be taking a lot of fish off the hooks.

To Paul Jacob and Norm Raffelson. Great fishermen who know how to put you "on fish." And not just that, they were inspiring for their love of the land, the water, and the fish that swim through it.

To Rabbi Harold Kushner for just being a good soul and listener, providing spot-on advice about writing and life. I always look forward to our talks and coffee.

To Boston College neuropsychology professor Joe Tecce and noted historian Anthony Rotundo for providing credibility and insight into the true human and psychological condition.

To Michael Belkin, my golfing friend, and one of the first to read earlier versions of *The Perfect Catch*. He doesn't even like to fish, but he knows the value of brotherly relationships and what makes for good reading. He wanted more from the relationship end of the writing and I hope I delivered it. One of these days I'll get him and his brother Nathan off the golf course and into a pond or stream. Actually we could fish and play golf in a special place that we each know quite well.

Gary Tanguay is my man. He is one of the best broadcasters I've ever seen. Nobody has a style like him and that's why it works. He's all of himself without being *full* of himself.

"I wanna go fishin' sooner!" It was one of his first and best pieces of advice when he read through early drafts. More than that, he pushed me and ultimately the whole family to make ourselves vulnerable, to the point where emotions were raw, but painfully honest. "I want tears, I want warts, I wanna know when you guys were really pissed off at each other. People *love* that," Gary boomed in that announcer's voice.

He was right. My father may not like it, but if Dad fusses, I'm blaming Tanguay. Everyone else does. Yeaaaahhh!

Susan Fay Spielman, my neighbor and middle school English teacher. This is the second time she's read through my books long before anyone else did. She makes me feel so good about my writing, but the grammar cop in her won't let me slide when my English gets a little too loose.

To my good friends Will and Hugh Reilly and the extended Reilly family. Thank you for being such good friends and endless reservoirs of entertainment and adventure. We should take another road trip for no good reason. It would be so much fun, but it would be tough to top that drive to North Carolina and back.

To Wayne Smolda for reading the manuscript and providing the sound advice as always, and for the friendship our family shares.

To Drew Yanno for encouraging more character development earlier in the book and providing direction about mixing present and past tense where appropriate.

To Josh Brogadir, fellow TV guy and aspiring author, who provided valuable geographic and technological advice, even though he portends to be an expert at neither.

To Chuck Little, my kama'aina Hawaii connection and regular reader of my writing. Thank you for keeping the Aloha Spirit alive in me and my words.

To Lisa Pelto at Concierge Marketing for her efforts to bring my writing dreams to life, and Sandra Wendel for her fine editing.

To my fellow members at Needham Sportsman's Club for their friendship and one sweet place to fish and hang out with my fishing buddies.

And to actor and literary agent Jacob Moore for suggesting a key writing tip that put an added urgency and energy into the writing.

ABOUT THE AUTHOR

Kevin Walsh is a seasoned anchor and reporter with Comcast SportsNet New England, and New England Cable News, divisions of NBC Universal. He's been in the locker rooms of and to The White House with World Series Winners and Stanley Cup Champions.

His first book, *The Marrow in Me* (Sports Challenge Network, 2009), tells the story of his becoming that one-in-a-million bone marrow donor match for a sixteen-year-old boy he'd never met. Not only did Kevin allow doctors to drill into his bones to harvest the marrow for transplant, he also ran a marathon to honor the boy who received it. There had never been a book written about bone marrow donation to a total stranger.

Kevin also wrote *Follow the Dog Home* (Sweet Tea Books, 2012) with his father, Bob, and ten-year-old daughter, Samantha. Described by *Publishers Weekly* as "quaint and most charming," *Follow the Dog Home* is the story of how Kevin's German Shepherd, Beverly, ultimately led him back to his father's long-lost childhood home sight unseen.

Kevin is married to Jean Walsh, and they are the parents of two young daughters: Samantha and Amanda.

Made in the USA
Charleston, SC
03 June 2013